INSIGHT COMPACT GUIDE

G000154874

Compact Guide: Vienna is the ultimate quick-reference guide to this fascinating destination. It tells you all you need to know about Vienna's attractions, from the imperial Hofburg to the famous buildings of the Ringstrasse, as well as reviewing its stunning collections of art and sampling the charm and comfort of its cafés.

This is one of 133 Compact Guides, combining the interests and enthusiasms of two of the world's best-known information providers: Insight Guides, whose innovative titles have set the standard for visual travel guides since 1970, and Discovery Channel, the world's premier source of nonfiction television programming.

APA PUBLICATIONS

Part of the Langenscheidt Publishing Group

Insight Compact Guide: Vienna

Written by: Dr Gerhard Sailer
English version by: Jane Michael
Revised by: Maria Lord
Photography by: Glyn Genin
Additional photography by: Bettmann/Corbis 13/1; Chris Hellier/Corbis
39/2; Wilhelm Klein 109; Maria Lord 20, 34, 36, 46, 60/1, 71/1, 72, 77/1,
83; Mark Read 47, 84, 85/1. 85/2, 94, 95, 100, 101/1, 101/2, 103; Vienna
Tourist Board 13/2, 41, 42, 93
Cover picture by: Rolf Richardson/Robert Harding Picture Library
Picture Editor: Hilary Genin
Maps: Polyglott/Buchhaupt

Editorial Director: Brian Bell
Managing Editor: Maria Lord

NO part of this book may be reproduced, stored in a retrieval system or
transmitted in any form or by any means (electronic, mechanical,
photocopying, recording or otherwise), without prior written permission of
Apa Publications. Brief text quotations with use of photographs are
exempted for book review purposes only.

CONTACTING THE EDITORS: As every effort is made to provide accurate
information in this publication, we would appreciate it if readers would
call our attention to any errors and omissions by contacting:
Apa Publications, PO Box 7910, London SE1 1WE, England.
Fax: (44 20) 7403 0290
e-mail: insight@apaguide.demon.co.uk

Information has been obtained from sources believed to be reliable,
but its accuracy and completeness, and the opinions based thereon,
are not guaranteed.

© 2003 APA Publications GmbH & Co. Verlag KG Singapore Branch, Singapore.

First Edition 1995; second edition 2003
Printed in Singapore by Insight Print Services (Pte) Ltd
Original edition © Polyglott-Verlag Dr Bolte KG, Munich

Distributed in the UK & Ireland by:
GeoCenter International Ltd
The Viables Centre, Harrow Way, Basingstoke,
Hampshire RG22 4BJ
Tel: (44 1256) 817-987, Fax: (44 1256) 817-988

Distributed in the United States by:
Langenscheidt Publishers, Inc.
46–35 54th Road, Maspeth, NY 11378
Tel: (1 718) 784-0055, Fax: (1 718) 784-0640

Worldwide distribution enquiries:
APA Publications GmbH & Co. Verlag KG (Singapore Branch)
38 Joo Koon Road, Singapore 628990
Tel: (65) 6865-1600, Fax: (65) 6861-6438

www.insightguides.com

Vienna

Introduction

Places

Culture

Practical Information

◁ **MuseumsQuartier (p77)** A huge new complex dedicated to 20th century and contemporary culture; it's home to Vienna's best contemporary art gallery, MUMOK, and the Leopold Museum, with a stunning collection of 20th-century Viennese painting.

▽ **MAK (p60)**
Vienna's museum of the applied arts is a treasure house of artefacts, from furniture to lace, all beautifully displayed by contemporary artists.

△ **Schönbrunn (p88)**
A vast palace, beloved of the later Hapsburgs, with beautiful grounds and the famous Gloriette.

△ **Belvedere (p62)**
Housed inside this jewel of a Baroque palace is an outstanding collection of paintings.

◁ **Secession (p69)**
This temple to art is the quintessential symbol of Viennese Art Nouveau.

△ **Hundertwasser (p59)** Love him or loathe him, the colourful buildings of Friedensreich Hundertwasser have provoked intense debate and made their mark on Vienna's environment.

△ **Hofburg (p40)** Centre of power of the Austrian empire for over 600 years, the Hofburg throws fascinating light on the Viennese court.

▽ **Staatsoper (p20)** One of the greatest opera houses in the world, with a distinguished history.

◁ **Stephansdom (p25)** A symbol of the city, the spire of Vienna's great Gothic cathedral soars above the surrounding rooftops.

▷ **Kunsthistorisches Museum (p73)** This superlative collection of art defies description. The paintings range from Titian to Velázquez, and Breugel to Rembrant. The collections of antiquities and decorative arts are equally impressive.

City of Nostalgia

Vienna, or Wien, the very name evokes a multitude of associations: a certain complacency amongst its citizens, a romantic trip in a fiacre past fine examples of Gothic, Baroque and Rococo architecture, amusements in the world-famous Prater crowned by a revolution of the big wheel, glittering evenings at the theatre or the opera, the benevolent omnipresence of the Emperor Francis Joseph gazing down on his subjects, and the beautiful blue Danube, along which pleasure boats chug so cheerfully.

And then, of course, there's the music: Viennese waltzes in the salons and parks, folk music in the *Heurigen*, golden clarity of the notes issuing from boyish throats, and the perfection of classical and modern cadences from the Vienna Philharmonic and Symphony Orchestras.

There is hardly a world capital which calls up images of so many clichés – stereotypes which reality cannot possibly hope to fulfil. 'Viennese blood' is anything but complacent, as the city's flourishing economy can testify; the fiacre drivers, famous for their sharp tongues, have to manoeuvre their team every day through a stinking sea of exhaust fumes; in Vienna at least, the Danube has never been either beautiful or blue; and only a last quantum of respect for the monarchy has prevented poor old Francis Joseph from suffering the same fate as Wolfgang Amadeus Mozart and his Mozartkugel.

Vienna still possesses a number of treasures, but they are mostly not well-known. Of course, every visitor should see the cathedral and experience the macabre shiver down the spine in the Capuchins' Crypt, and many will file past the endless glass display cases containing priceless jewels in the various state museums. But Vienna is also a surprisingly good place for tracking down modern art: Egon Schiele, Gustav Klimt, Otto Wagner and Adolf Loos. For this city doesn't just cling nostalgically to its past, but makes room for contemporary art – as can be seen in MUMOK and the imposing Alfred Hrdlicka monument on the

> **City of musicians**
> Vienna can lay claim to being the most influential musical city of the Austro-German world. Over a period of 200 years it was at the vanguard of musical thought, from Classicism to atonality. Its famous inhabitants included: the 'first Viennese school' of Haydn, Mozart and Beethoven; Schubert, Brahms, Bruckner, Wolf and Mahler; and the 'second Viennese school' of Schoenberg, Berg and Webern.

Opposite: a fiacre's lamp
Below: in the Schloss Schönbrunn garden

Albertinaplatz. It is also fascinating to contemplate St Rupert's Church, a Romanesque jewel modestly tucked away from the main tourist track, but surrounded by bars and restaurants that are popular with the Viennese.

Vienna is, in fact, not at all as you expect it to be. Surprises await you around every corner.

LOCATION AND SIZE

The Secession Building

The volcanic intrusion of the Vienna Basin forms a gap in the vast mountain chain of the Alps and the Carpathians, which separate Central and Southern Europe. The Danube, the second-largest river in Europe, wends its way through this gap. In earliest times, it served as a meeting place of travel and trading routes: the Danube formed the most important link between East and West, with the 'Amber Road' from the Baltic leading south to the Adriatic. Vienna owes its development largely to its location at this early crossroads.

The metropolitan area covers approximately 415sq km (160sq miles). Within the city itself there are considerable variations of altitude: the Prater area is about 152m (500ft) above sea level, whilst the district of Favoriten on the Laaerberg lies at 255m (836ft).

The city has a population of approximately 1.6 million inhabitants (about 20 percent of the total population of Austria), of whom 89 percent are Roman Catholics.

CLIMATE

Vienna's location to the east of the Alps, Europe's major climatic barrier, results in the city's climate being influenced by two different climatic zones. The northern European–Baltic climate brings cool summers and mild winters, whilst the southeast European arid climate is responsible for warm summers and harsh winters. This encounter between two weather systems produces the typical Viennese climate, which is mild and pleasant. Periods of excessive cold or heat seldom last long. The average temperature is approximately –2°C (28°F) in January and 22°C (72°F) in July. The average minimum temperature is –20°C (–4°F) and the maximum is 33°C (91°F).

Another important factor is the Wiener Lüfterl, an almost constant light breeze from the west or northwest, which means that, even in midsummer, the evenings remain pleasantly cool.

POPULATION

The basis of Vienna's population was formed by a Bavarian settlement in the Middle Ages, although the local residents started to assert their independence from Upper Germany and Bavaria as early as the 14th century. Reflecting its multinational population, Vienna became the capital of a large and diverse empire. The Slavic, and in particular the Czech, element came to predominate, combining with the Magyar and Romance elements to produce the cosmopolitan mixture which characterises the city's present-day population. Many of their traits can be traced back to these early encounters: their well-known talent for music and dance, their affected nonchalance and casual manner, the meticulous attention to external appearances and their sureness of touch when it comes to good taste.

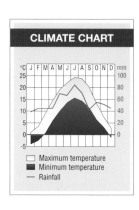

CLIMATE CHART

☐ Maximum temperature
■ Minimum temperature
– Rainfall

Imperial remains
The Hoch- und Deutschmeister (Vienna Household Regiment), founded in 1696, drew its members from amongst the former Teutonic Order of Knights (hence the name). Popularly known as the Emperor's Noble Lads, their uniform (blue trousers and blue revers) is still worn today by the Deutschmeister band.

On Schwarzenbergplatz

THE CITY STRUCTURE

Vienna is not only the capital of Austria; it is also a province in its own right. For administrative purposes, the city is divided into 23 districts, which are generally referred to by means of Roman numerals. The city centre (I) lies between the Danube Canal and the former city walls, and this is where most of the public buildings and bank headquarters are to be found, as well as the majority of the tourist sights.

Below: a Ringstrasse tram
Bottom: view over the city,
with the Karlskirche to the left

The city centre is surrounded by a ring of inner boroughs (II–IX), which are numbered clockwise. Baroque palaces and churches rise up here and there along the Classical main streets, but with increasing distance from the centre the more modest residential districts gradually take over. In the Leopoldstadt, the Landstrasse district and the Wieden there are tradesmen's premises and small factories; part of Landstrasse is also the diplomatic quarter. Margareten is a working-class district, in marked contrast to Mariahilf and Neubau, both of which house large firms.

The Josefstadt has long enjoyed a reputation as the home of officials, and the district of Alsergrund includes a large number of hospitals and the university *(see page 84)*.

Beyond the ring road are the outer boroughs (X–XX). These districts are characterised in part by large communal buildings erected after 1918

and 1945 to provide housing, and in part by elegant residential areas or the unpretentious settlements that have grown up around medieval churches. Favoriten, Simmering and Meidling are predominantly working-class. Hietzing is characterised by little Biedermeier mansions and a touch of exclusiveness; Penzing is also mainly middle-class. Rudolfsheim-Fünfhaus, Ottakring and Hernals have a reputation as typical working-class areas, whilst Währing and Döbling are full of villas; some districts of Döbling (Grinzing, Sievering, Neistift and Nussdorf) have preserved their typical village character.

INTERNATIONAL VIENNA

Apart from its reputation as a popular venue for international congresses, Vienna is also the seat of a number of United Nations (UN) organisations. The IAEO (the International Atomic Energy Organisation), the UNIDO (International Industrial Development Organisation) and a number of other bodies are in the International Centre, known as UNO City, housed on the left bank of the Danube.

THE VIENNESE AND DEATH

The Viennese have always had a unique relationship with death; a fact to which the countless melancholy, sometimes macabre, Viennese songs testify. From Baroque times the Viennese laid great store by a good funeral. Forming part of the ceremonial were the *Pompfüneberer*, official mourners in black costumes inspired by the Spanish court, who accompanied the funeral procession. The dimensions of the additional spectacle (flowers, candles, etc) were determined by the class of funeral (magnificent, superior and six further categories), and by the financial situation of the deceased's family. This was seen to excellent effect in 1989 at the funeral of Empress Zita, wife of the last Hapsburg ruler, Karl I. Nowadays this magnificence is rare as few can afford to put on such a show *(see also page 99).*

Etiquette
Compliments are often heard in the city, for the Viennese seldom miss an opportunity for making a flattering remark. Such expressions as 'I kiss your hand, Madam' or 'I am honoured', or 'Please do us the honour again soon' are commonplace in Vienna, in addition to the well-known greeting *Grüss Gott* (God be with you) and the familiar *Servus* (Your servant). Nor has the practice of kissing hands disappeared.

A flower stall on the corner of the Stadtpark

Psychoanalysis and Freud

The life of the hugely influential, and still controversial, psychoanalyst Sigmund Freud was inextricably linked with Vienna. Born into a Jewish family in Freiberg, Moravia (now in the Czech Republic), on 6 May 1856, Freud was only 4 years old when his family moved to Vienna in 1860. After studying medicine at the University of Vienna and working at Vienna General Hospital, he went to study under the brilliant neuropathologist Jean Martin Charcot in Paris. Charcot's work on hysteria made a great impact on the young Freud, and on his return to Vienna in 1886 he began to treat nervous conditions in his own patients.

It has been pointed out that it may well have been only in the febrile atmosphere of *fin-de-siècle* Vienna that Freud would have found both the patients and the intellectual milieu in which to develop his ideas. Freud himself, however, seems to have had a love-hate relationship with the city; although he spent much of his life there, he is reported to have 'detested' the place.

His own work on hysteria, based on case studies undertaken with Josef Breuer (published in 1895), came to the conclusion that neurosis was caused by trauma. He soon moved beyond this theory when, from 1896, he began to develop his ground-breaking practice of psychoanalysis.

Brought on in part by his own rigorous self-analysis, this led to his formualtion of the concepts of infantile sexuality and, famously, the Oedipus complex. In a string of publications, Freud went on to write on dreams (1899), sexuality (1905), incest (*Totem and Taboo*, 1912–13), and, in 1923, on the structure of the mind by introducing the concepts of the ego and the id.

His reputation continued to grow and his work began to have profound influence beyond the sphere of neuroscience, particularly in music, painting and literature. However, this international reputation did not prevent persecution. With the arrival of the Nazis in Vienna in 1938, Freud and his family, as (albeit atheist) Jews, were forced to flee to England. He died in London on 23 September 1939.

Viennese porcelain
The Augarten porcelain factory was founded by Du Paquier in 1718 and taken over by the state in 1744. Since then, a blue coat of arms has been the trademark of the famous porcelain. Artistically speaking, the most important periods of production were the early years and the end of the 18th and the beginning of the 19th century, when the company developed its own Rococo, Classical and Biedermeier styles.

The Hundertwasserhaus

FASCHING AND SOCIETY BALLS

Vienna is famous for its pre-Lenten *(Fasching)* elegant society balls, which have their antecedent in the balls held at the court from 1877 onwards. The most exclusive balls include the Philharmonikerball (held at the Musikverein), the Technikercercle and Kaiserball at the Hofburg, Campagnereiterball, the Lawyers' Ball and the Jägerball (where the guests wear traditional costume). However, the best-known, and most expensive, is the Opernball held at the Staatsoper. This attracts a great number of the rich and famous, and is a place to see and be seen.

Not all the balls are so expensive or difficult to get into, and many of them are for particular professions. Of particular interest are the artists' masked balls known as *Gschnasfeste*.

Below: Sigmund Freud
Bottom: at the Opernball

THE SPANISCHE RIETSCHULE

One of Vienna's best-known attractions is the Spanische Rietschule (Spanish Riding School), founded in the 1570s. Home to the white Lipizzaner horses (named after the stud farm near Trieste where they originated), this is the last place where the art of classical dressage is still maintained. The school, part of the imperial court, moved into its present splendid Baroque building in 1735 (*see page 41*; also www.spanische-reitschule.com).

HISTORICAL HIGHLIGHTS

c. 2000 BC Indo-Germanic tribes settle in the Vienna area.

c. 1000 BC Illyrian settlements are to be found on the slopes of the Vienna Woods.

c. 400 BC The settlement of Vindobona, thought to refer to the Vinides, a Celtic tribe, develops on the site of the present Hoher Markt.

15 BC Roman legions occupy what is now Austria. The Danube marks the northern frontier of the Roman Empire, and the Vienna Basin becomes part of Pannonia. The Roman legionary camp of Vindobona lay within the present city centre. The civilian town (with approximately 20,000 inhabitants) lay in the Belvedere district.

AD 180 The Roman Emperor Mark Aurelius dies at Vindobona.

c. 280 The Romans introduce viticulture to the Danube region.

c. 425 The Huns under Attila invade Pannonia. In 450 'Vindomina' is mentioned by the historian Jordanes in his history of the Goths.

8th century The Bavarians reach the Vienna Woods. In 788, Charlemagne deposes Tassilo III, Duke of Bavaria, repulses the advancing Avars and founds the Carolingian Empire in 799.

881 The name 'Wenia' occurs for the first time in the Salzburg Annals.

c. 960 The Babenbergs become margraves of the Eastern March (mentioned in records in 996 as 'Ostarichi'), which also includes 'Wiennis'. Margrave Leopold III the Saintly (1095–1136) builds a castle on the Leopoldsberg.

1137 Vienna receives its town charter.

1156 The Eastern March becomes an independent duchy. Henry II Jasomirgott moves his residence from Klosterneuburg to Vienna.

1194–8 The poet Walther von der Vogelweide lives at the ducal court in Vienna.

1221 Vienna receives municipal and staple rights, requiring foreign merchants to offer their goods for sale in Vienna.

1246 The last of the Babenbergs, Duke Frederick II, is killed in the Battle of the Leitha against the Hungarians. Control of Austria passes to King Otokar of Bohemia.

1278 Otokar is killed in the Battle of the Marchfeld against King Rudolf I von Habsburg. Rudolf founds the Habsburg dynasty which will rule the country until 1918. During the same year the 'Vienna Penny' appears for the first time bearing the city's coat of arms: a cross on a triangular shield. Around this time, the city enjoys rapid expansion in the wake of the crusades and is surrounded by a fortifying wall.

1326 and 1327 Fires partially destroy the city.

1349 Vienna's population is almost wiped out by the plague.

1365 The University of Vienna is founded.

1438 The Austrian Duke Albert V becomes King Albert II of Germany. From this point until 1806, except for short interruptions, the rulers of the Holy Roman Empire resided in Vienna.

1469 Frederick III makes the city a bishopric. St Stephen's Church becomes a cathedral.

1485–90 King Mathias Corvinus of Hungary resides in Vienna.

1493 Emperor Maximilian I drives the Hungarians out of Austria. During his reign the Reformation reaches the country.

1526 King Louis II of Hungary and Bohemia dies fighting the Turks in the Battle of Mohács. His kingdom is ceded to Austria.

1529 Vienna is besieged by the Turks.

1618–48 The Thirty Years' War. In 1623 the Counter-Reformation begins in Vienna. From 1645 Swedish troops are stationed in Austria. An absolute monarchy replaces the Estates as the ruler of the Habsburg territories.

1683 The Turks lay siege to Vienna once more; on their retreat they leave behind them a 'gift' of lasting value: coffee.

1683–1736 Prince Eugène of Savoy assumes command of the Imperial Army. Leading campaigns against the Turks and the French, he reasserts the empire's position as a major power.

1698 The present city districts II–IX and XX are incorporated in the precincts charter of Emperor Leopold I and surrounded by the Linienwall fortifications (1704).

1740–80 Maria Theresa removes the power of the nobility. A centralised system of government makes Vienna a world metropolis.

1804 Francis II is appointed Emperor Francis I of Austria.

1805 Napoleon I lays siege to the city. Succumbing to pressure, Francis II abandons the title of Holy Roman Emperor on 6 August 1806.

1809 Napoleon besieges Vienna again and takes up residence in Schloss Schönbrunn. Archduke Charles defeats him at Aspern, near Vienna. However, Napoleon forces the Austrians to accept a truce after his victory at the Battle of Wagram. Francis Napoleon, Duke of Reichstadt, is born after Napoleon's marriage (1810) to Archduchess Marie Louise.

1814–15 After the fall of Napoleon, the Congress of Vienna is held under the aegis of Count (later Prince) Metternich.

1848 Revolt against Metternich's rule forces his resignation. On 2 December Ferdinand I abdicates in favour of his nephew, Francis Joseph.

1848–1916 Reign of Francis Joseph I. By 1857 Vienna has a population of 600,000 and has spread far beyond the original city limits. The old city fortifications and city walls are torn down and the Ringstrasse built along the line of the walls. In 1867 the state becomes the dual monarchy of Austria-Hungary. In 1890 the Linienwall fortifications are demolished.

1897–1910 The leader of the Christian Socialist Party, Karl Lueger, becomes mayor. Vienna develops into a modern metropolis.

1918 World War I ends; dual monarchy collapses. Austria becomes a republic on 12 November.

1920 Vienna becomes an independent province with a Social Democrat mayor.

1938 The *Anschluss*: Austria becomes the *Ostmark* within the Third German Reich. Vienna becomes a *Reichsgau* with 26 districts.

1945 Shortly before the end of World War II, Vienna is the scene of heavy fighting. The Russians occupy the city on 11 April, later followed by the other Allies. Vienna begins reconstruction.

1951–65 In addition to new housing and the implementation of welfare services, Vienna introduces a modern transport system.

1955 The treaty signed in Belvedere Palace between Austria and the Allied Powers guarantees Austria's sovereignty and neutrality.

1979 The International Centre handed over to the United Nations, making Vienna the third United Nations city, after New York and Geneva.

1995 Austria becomes a member of the EU.

1999 After a general election, the far-right Freedom Party becomes part of the government, provoking huge demonstrations and condemnation from foreign governments.

2002 The Danube rises to dangerous levels and parts of the city are flooded.

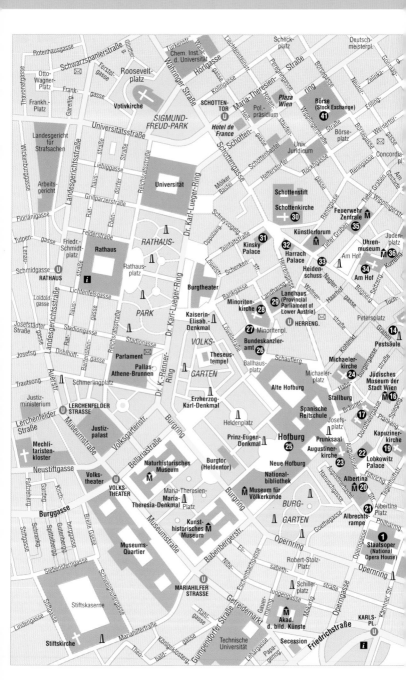

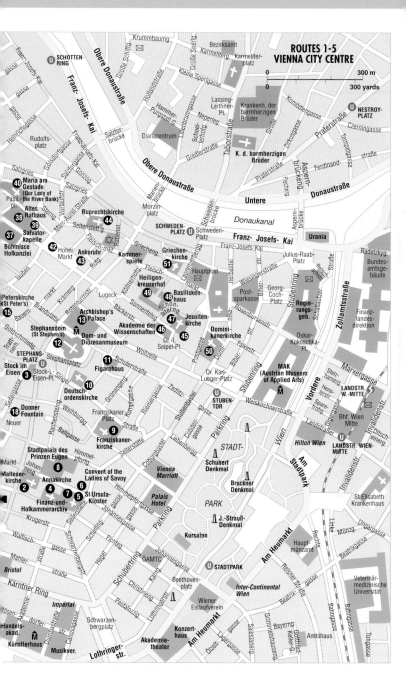

ROUTES 1-5
VIENNA CITY CENTRE

0   300 m
0   300 yards

Map
on pages
18–19

1: Staatsoper to Stephansdom

There are two possible routes from the Staatsoper to the city centre: firstly, directly along Vienna's high street, Kärntner Strasse, or alternatively, by taking a detour through the historic alleys of the Kärntner and Weihburg districts.

THE STAATSOPER

At the Opera crossroads at the intersection of the Ringstrasse and the Kärntner Strasse stands the ★★★ **Staatsoper ❶**. (National Opera House; Conducted tours 35 mins July–Aug daily 10am, 11am, 1pm, 2pm, 3pm; Sept–Jul usually 2pm, 3pm, closed intermittently, tel: 514 44 2613.) The former Hofoperntheater (Court Opera), one of the leading opera houses in the world, was built between 1861 and 1869 in Renaissance style to a design by August von Siccardsburg and Eduard van der Nüll. Its first season, in 1869, opened with Mozart's *Don Giovanni*. Almost completely burnt out in 1945 after suffering a direct hit during a bombing raid, the opera house was rebuilt under the direction of Erich Boltenstern, using the original plans. The safety curtain (decorated with a picture of Orpheus and Eurydice) finally rose again on 5 November 1955 with Karl Böhm conducting *Fidelio* for the re-inauguration.

Local passions

Herbert von Karajan experienced the involvement of the citizens of Vienna when he directed the opera company between 1956 and 1964. He once commented that he had to contend with 1.6 million co-directors, all determined to teach him how to run an opera company.

The Staatsoper facade from the Ringstrasse

The main facade of the opera house, facing the Ringstrasse, is elaborately decorated. The frescoes on the middle loggia (depicting scenes from Mozart's *Magic Flute*), and the scenes from the opera in the foyer, were the work of Moritz von Schwind. In the arches of the loggia are allegorical bronze statues depicting Heroism, Drama, Imagination, Art and Love. The figures on the marble fountain beside the opera house represent (left) an allegory of Music and (right) the Lorelei.

Star Attraction
● **Staatsoper**

Below: the Lobmeyr shop-front on Kärntner Strasse
Bottom: a relief in the Malteserkirche

MALTESERKIRCHE

Walk down the Kärntner Strasse, now a shopping street but mentioned as early as 1257 in records as *Strata Carinthianorum*. On the right you will pass the street's oldest building (No 41), part of the **former Esterházy palace** (17th and 18th centuries) before coming to the **Malteserkirche ❷** (Church of the Knights of Malta). The church of the independent knightly order, which by 1217 had established a *dépendance* here as the Order of the Knights of St John, is a Gothic building dating from 1450 to which a Classical facade was added from 1806 to 1808. The most noticeable feature of the Empire-style interior is the high altar, with its statues of St Peter and St Paul and *The Baptism of Christ* by Johann Georg Schmidt. Of interest, too, are the coats of arms of the Grand Masters of the Order in the choir and the monument to the Grand Master La Valette (1557–68), erected in 1806.

STOCK IM EISEN

On the left-hand corner of the Kärntner Strasse and the little square known as Stock-im-Eisen-Platz, which served as the city's horse fair until 1327, stands the **Stock im Eisen ❸** (iron ring). The stump of a spruce tree, first mentioned in 1533, is probably the remains of a forest which once grew here. Wandering blacksmiths and locksmiths were required to hammer a nail into the tree trunk. The iron ring surrounding the stump, now protected behind a perspex casing is – according to legend – sealed with a lock which cannot be opened.

Map on pages 18–19

THROUGH THE WEIHBURG DISTRICT

Turning right off Kärntner Strasse, by the Esterházy Palace mentioned above, and entering the narrow Annagasse, you will come to the ★ **Annakirche** ❹ (Church of St Anne). Originally a Gothic building dating from 1320, the church was rebuilt in the Baroque style in 1747. At the same time, Daniel Gran created the three ceiling frescoes (the *Immaculate Conception*, the *Redemption* and the *Apotheosis*), as well as the picture of the *Holy Family* over the high altar. The *Triple Portrait of St Anne* (c. 1505) sculpture adorns the altar of the chapel opposite the entrance; ascribed by some experts to Veit Stoss, the masterpiece is considered by others to be the work of the Master of the Maurer Altar in Mauer, not far from Melk.

The Haas Haus

Opposite the iron ring, in contrast, stands the modern ★ **Haas House** (1990), built according to plans by Hans Hollein. The large, partially mirrored, curved exterior is supposed to represent a 'hinge' between Graben and Stephansplatz. The decoration of the interior is expensive and lavish; the intention was to create an environment for exclusive boutiques. The building also houses the expensive Aioli and Do&Co restaurant and café.

FORMER URSULINE CONVENT

Turn left at the Seilerstätte, and then left again into Johannesgasse (named after the Knights of St John who were once resident here). The Vienna Music Academy now occupies the **St Ursula Kloster** ❺ (convent). The sprawling building also includes the Ursulakirche (Ursuline Church; 1665–75), with a fine Rococo interior, a **collection of religious folk art**, and the former convent apothecary.

The Haas Haus seen from Kärntner Strasse

Opposite stands an example of late Viennese Baroque architecture – the **Convent of the Ladies of Savoy** ❻. The figure of the *Immaculata* (1768) adorning the facade of the building, first mentioned in 1770, and the fountain in the inner courtyard, *The Widow of Zarephath* (1766–70), are both masterpieces by Franz Xaver Messerschmidt.

Next door, at No 6, is the oldest archive building in Europe, the ★ **Finanz-und-Hofkammer-archiv** ❼ (Archives of the Court Chamberlain), established in 1578. Between 1832 and 1856, the writer Franz Grillparzer was the director of the archives; his office on the fourth floor is open to the public Mon–Fri 9am–2.30pm. The oldest manuscript in the archive, the land deeds for a monastery, dates from 1170 and is signed with 3 small dots by the Holy Roman Emperor.

Below: the Holy Family in the Annakirche
Bottom: sign for the religious folk art collection

THE WINTER PALACE

Further along (No 5) lies the Palais Questenberg-Kaunitz (1701–23; today part of the Ministry of Finance; no access to the public), in which Austria's most famous general, Prince Eugène of Savoy, died in 1736.

The building is linked by a courtyard to the building at No 8 Himmelpfortgasse, since 1848 also a part of the Ministry of Finance, the ★ **Stadtpalais der Prinzen Eugen** ❽ (Winter Palace of Prince Eugène). Built in 1697–8 by Johann Bernhard Fischer von Erlach, the palace was extended from 1708 to 1728 by Lukas von Hildebrandt. The massive facade is characterised by three ornamental entrances, decorated by reliefs extending to the balconies adorned by cherubs, and windows decorated by weapons and sculptures.

The magnificent staircase was also executed in accordance with plans drawn up by Fischer von Erlach. The massive giants' statues were the work of Giovanni Giuliani; the stucco work representing the *Labours of Hercules* is by Santino Bussi. The oil paintings on the ceiling are by Louis Dorigny. (Only the foyer and staircase are open to the public; ask permission from the guards at the entrance, Mon–Fri.)

Map on pages 18–19

The Mozart trail

Passing along the narrow Blutgasse (on the right, before the Teutonic church) you will then arrive at the ★★ **Figarohaus** ⓫ (Mozart's house; open Tues–Sun 9am–6pm, closed 1 Jan, 1 May, 25 Dec). Wolfgang Amadeus Mozart composed *The Marriage of Figaro* and several other works between 1784 and 1787 whilst living on the first floor of this house. Now a museum dedicated to the Mozart family, it has displays of facsimile scores, paintings and listening points. The museum ends – a little bizarrely – in what appears to be a marble-clad shrine to the composer.

The Dutch winged altar in the Teutonic Church

FRANZISKANERKIRCHE

Proceeding along the Rauhensteingasse, in which Wolfgang Amadeus Mozart died in 1791 (there is a commemorative plaque on No 8), turn right into the Weihburggasse; the name derives from the 13th-century *Weichburg*, which in those days adjoined the judicial district of the city. This opens out into the Franziskanerplatz, with its Moses Fountain (1798, by Johann Martin Fischer), and the ★ **Franziskanerkirche** ❾ (Church of the Franciscans; 1603–11). Originally part of a convent built in 1383 for lay sisters and later handed over to the Franciscans, the church is a blend of Gothic and Northern Renaissance styles, especially striking in the gables adorning the facade. The interior dates from the 18th century; the third altar on the right depicts a *Crucifixion* by Carlo Carlone; the high altar, designed by Andrea Pozzi in 1707, surrounds a late-Gothic Madonna (15th-century). Of the altars in the south aisle, the second (the *Martyrdom of St John Capistrano*, by FX Wagenschön) and the third (the *Immaculata*, from the school of Rottmayr) deserve attention.

DEUTSCHORDERNSKIRCHE

North of the church lies Singerstrasse on which there are two 18th-century palaces. Directly opposite is the **Palais Rottal** (1750–4) and, to the left, the **Palais Neupauer-Breuner** (1715–16).

Further to the left stands the ★ **Deutschordernskirche** ❿ (Church of the Teutonic Order; open Mon–Sun 7am–6pm, guided tours by arrangement, tel: 512 106515). The Teutonic Order, resident in Vienna from about 1200, added this church (built 1326–75) to their existing buildings (c. 1220). Of particular note are a Dutch winged altar (c. 1500) and several 16th-, 17th- and 18th-century memorials. In the House of the Teutonic Order next door (the present building dates from the 18th century) is a fine ★ **Treasury** (open Mon and Thur 10am–noon, Wed and Fri 3pm–5pm, Sat 10am–noon, 3pm–5pm).

Continuing along Singerstrasse brings you out onto **Stephansplatz**.

STEPHANSDOM

Dominating the square is ★★★ **Stephansdom** ⓬ (St Stephen's Cathedral; open Mon–Sat 6am–10pm; Sun and public holidays 7am–10pm; guided tours in English 3.45pm daily, 1 Apr–31 Oct).

Star Attractions
- **Figarohaus**
- **Stephansdom**

CATHEDRAL HISTORY

The city's landmark is one of the most notable German Gothic religious monuments. From 1137 to 1147 Heinrich II Jasomirgott had a Romanesque church built on this site; between 1230 and 1276 the original building was replaced by a masterpiece of late-Romanesque architecture. Between 1304 and 1340 a Gothic choir was added to the nave.

The builder of the present cathedral was Duke Rudolf IV the Founder, who laid the foundation stone in 1359. Michael Chnab, Hans von Prachatitz and Hans Puchsbaum were responsible for the South Tower and the nave, completed in 1455. The construction of the North Tower was basically abandoned in 1511, although it is unknown whether this was owing to aesthetic or financial grounds. Since 1496, St Stephen's has been a cathedral; since 1723 it has been the centre of an archdiocese. After a devastating fire towards the end of World War II, the building was renovated; work was completed in 1952.

Below: a late-Gothic lantern
Bottom: Stephansdom

Map on pages 18–19

TOUR OF THE CATHEDRAL

The **Riesentor** (Giants' Doorway), a round-arched, late-Romanesque doorway (c. 1240) with rich decoration, is the main entrance. Above the columns is a frieze of human and animal sculptures (the Evil of the World), above which can be seen the figures of the Apostles and, on the outside, seated likenesses of the master builders. Within the tympanum is a Christ in Majesty. In the recesses are late-Romanesque statues: Samson fighting the lions, a griffon, a seated judge, St Stephen (c. 1500) and two lions. The Gothic west window, added above the Giants' Doorway, dates from later.

Above are the **Heidentürme** (Towers of the Pagans; 65m/213ft) which acquired their Gothic countenance at a later date. The figures adorning the baldachins on the side extensions represent Albert IV (1395–1405) and his wife Joanna.

Around the corner, past a 15th-century late-Gothic lantern, are the ruins of the **tombstone of Nithart Fuchs**, the 'merry chancellor' of Duke Otto the Cheerful, who died in 1334. Nearby, beside the Cantor's Door, is a statue of the crucified Christ dating from 1435.

St Stephen's Tower staircase (418 steps) begins in the sacristy. The city's fire lookouts – and during the Turkish sieges, military observers – used to keep watch from the guardroom in the tower (open 9am–5.30pm daily).

On the southeastern corner of the exterior are the **Straub monument** (1520), a Renaissance tomb relief showing Christ taking leave of his mother, surrounded by medallions depicting scenes from the Passion of Christ, and the late-Gothic **Lackner monument** dating from 1502, with a relief of the Mount of Olives.

Baroque additions to a Gothic pulpit

THE EASTERN EXTERIOR

The eastern end of the Cathedral has a series of **late-Gothic frescoes** depicting the Passion of Christ (c. 1500), **three reliefs** showing scenes from the Passion (early 15th century), and Josef Danhauser's All Souls fresco (1826). In the middle is the **'Christ of the Toothache'**, a large statue of the crucified Christ (c. 1400); the name supposedly derives from the 'miraculous' healing of an unbeliever's toothache.

The **Gothic stone pulpit** (c. 1430) is where the Franciscan monk John Capestrano called the citizens to join the crusade against the Turks in 1451. Its Baroque additions date from 1737.

Next to the pulpit is the **Crypt chapel** (1752), with a staircase leading down to the catacombs. Close by a monument can be found dating from around 1520 which has a large sandstone relief of *The Last Judgement*, and the **Renaissance monument** (1508) to Konrad Celtis, the founder of German humanism.

THE INTERIOR

Entering the Dom, the best overall view of the spectacular interior is from beneath the **organ loft**. The nave is 101m (331ft) long; the total width of the three naves is 34m (111ft). The vaulting, 27m (88ft) high, is borne by 18 sets of pillars, which were constructed between 1435 and 1480.

Steffl

St Stephen's Tower, affectionately known as 'Steffl', is regarded as the supreme example of Gothic tower construction. It was begun in 1365 by Michael Chnab, and completed in 1433 by Hans von Prachatitz. The octagonal helm roof soars in three stages towards the summit, which is formed by a finial and a bronze ball with a two-headed eagle. Under the tower lies the Prime Door, with figures of the Evangelists and a Madonna (c. 1420).

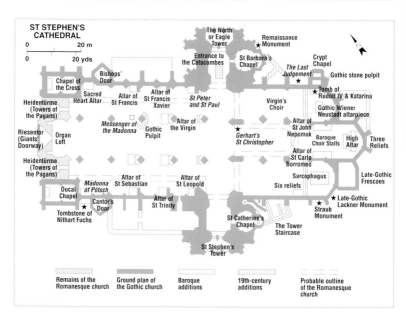

ST STEPHEN'S CATHEDRAL

0 — 20 m
0 — 20 yds

The North or Eagle Tower
Entrance to the Catacombs
St Barbara's Chapel
Remaissance Monument ★
Crypt Chapel
The Last Judgement ★
Gothic stone pulpit

Chapel of the Cross
Bishops' Door
Sacred Heart Altar
Altar of St Francis
Altar of St Francis Xavier
St Peter and St Paul
Virgin's Choir
★ Tomb of Rudolf IV & Katarina
Gothic Wiener Neustadt altarpiece

Heidentürme (Towers of the Pagans)
Messenger of the Madonna
Altar of the Virgin
Gothic Pulpit
Altar of St John Nepomuk

Riesentor (Giants' Doorway)
Organ Loft
★ *Gerhart's St Christopher*
Baroque Choir Stalls
High Altar
Three Reliefs

Heidentürme (Towers of the Pagans)
Altar of St Carlo Borromeo

Ducal Chapel
Madonna of Pötsch
Altar of St Sebastian
Altar of St Leopold
Sarcophagus
Six reliefs
Late-Gothic Frescoes

Cantor's Door
Altar of St Trinity
★ Late-Gothic Lackner Monument

Tombstone of Nithart Fuchs
St Catherine's Chapel
The Tower Staircase
★ Straub Monument

St Stephen's Tower

Remains of the Romanesque church | Ground plan of the Gothic church | Baroque additions | 19th-century additions | Probable outline of the Romanesque church

Map
on pages
18–19

Tower bell

The North or Eagle Tower (60m/197ft) was begun in 1450 in accordance with plans drawn up by Hans Puchsbaum; work came to a halt in 1511. In 1579 Hans Sapphoy completed the tower with an octagonal belfry. Beneath the tower is the richly carved Eagle Door. Since 1957 the tower has housed the Pummerin, one of the largest bells in the world. Cast in 1711 from the metal of captured Turkish cannon, the bell originally hung in the Steffl. In April 1945 it fell to the ground and shattered. It was recast in 1951. (The lift to the top of the tower is in the north aisle.)

Looking down the nave of Stephansdom

The **Ducal Chapel** to the right has 14th-century statues of St Ludmilla (holding a cord and a palm frond) and St Afra (holding the branch of a tree), as well as the 'Domestic Madonna'. The carved altar of St Valentine dates from 1507.

Beneath the altar baldachin (1510–15, by Gregor Hauser and Jörg Oexl) stands the *Madonna of Pötsch*, a Carpatho-Russian masterpiece. Beside this, the **Cantor's Door** (1440–50) by Hans Puchsbaum, once the entrance used by male visitors, is decorated with sculptures of male saints, and, to the left, Rudolf I and his wife Katharina.

THE CHAPEL OF THE CROSS

On the other side of the nave, the **Chapel of the Cross**, visible through a fine Baroque railing (1736), has had Prince Eugene of Savoy's tomb on the left-hand side since 1754.

The **Sacred Heart Altar** is surrounded by a baldachin (1434) by Hans von Prachatitz, and beside it, the **Bishops' Door** (c. 1515) was the entrance for female visitors (now the Dom shop). The sculptures depict female saints, Duke Albert III and his wife Elizabeth. Further on JM Rottmayr painted the altarpiece (1715) for the **Altar of St Francis**.

The *Messenger of the Madonna*, an early Gothic statue now encased in plastic, can be found on the rail of the **Gothic pulpit**, carved by Pilgram

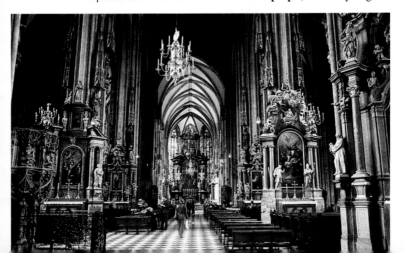

around 1500. The stairs are adorned with toads
and lizards (symbols of evil), which a dog (symbol of good) prevents from ascending. On the
balustrade are (from right to left): St Ambrose, St
Jerome, Pope Gregory the Great and St Augustine. The man looking out of the window at the
foot of the ramp is a self-portrait of Pilgram.

The **Altar of St Francis Xavier** (1690) portrays the saint preaching to Africans. Next to the
altar is the lift entrance up to the *Pummerin* tower
(open daily Apr–Jun, Sept–Oct 9am–6pm; Jul–
Aug 9am–6.30pm; Nov–Mar 8.30am–7pm).

At the base of the late-Gothic organ (1513) is
a self-portrait of the artist, Anton Pilgram, with
the artist's monogram beneath.

Of the two Baroque altars, the painting *St Peter
and St Paul* (1677) is by Tobias Pock, and the
Altar of the Virgin has a portrait (1493) reputed
to have miraculous powers.

By **St Barbara's Chapel** is the **entrance to the
catacombs**, with the grave of Rudolf IV, the Bishops' Vault and copper urns containing the internal organs of the Habsburgs (tours daily every 15
to 30 mins Mon–Fri 10am–11.30am, 1.30pm–
4.30pm; Sun and public holidays 1.30pm–4.30pm).

THE VIRGIN'S CHOIR

The **Virgin's Choir** has five red marble tombs
(the foremost reputedly designed by Loy Hering
for Bishop Georg Slatkonia in 1522) which are
opposite the **Tomb of Rudolf IV and his wife
Katharina** (1378). In the upper section of the central shrine of the **Gothic Wiener Neustadt altarpiece** (1447) is a Coronation of the Virgin; the
lower section depicts the Virgin, St Barbara and
St Catherine. The inner wings depict the lives of
the Virgin and Christ.

The **High Altar**, carved of black marble by
Johann Jakob Pock (1640–7), includes the *Martyrdom of St Stephen* painted on pewter panels by
Tobias Pock. The **Baroque choir stalls** (1647)
have busts of various bishops. Above, to the right,
is the Musicians' Choir, and to the left the Imperial Oratory.

*Below: Pilgram's pulpit, and
(bottom) his self-portrait
beneath a late-Gothic organ*

Map on pages 18–19

Next are the two Baroque altars; the first of **St John Nepomuk** (1723) with a painting (1772) by Johann Martin Schmidt, and the second of **St Carlo Borromeo** (1728), with an altarpiece (1783) by Wolfgang Köpp. On the pillar in the Central Choir is Gerhaert's *St Christopher* (c. 1470).

The **Sarcophagus** (1467–1513) for Emperor Frederick III was designed by Nicolaus Gerhaert van Leyden, who was also responsible for the tombstone with the figure of the emperor in coronation robes. Max Valmet and Michael Tichter executed the side panels. Beside this, in the Apostle's Choir, are six noteworthy **reliefs** (c. 1520) depicting scenes of the Passion.

St Catherine's Chapel has a baptismal font (1481) by Ulrich Auer. The reliefs surrounding the basin depict Christ, St John the Baptist and the Apostles; those on the pedestal, the Evangelists, and those on the font cover, the sacraments. On the knob is a representation of the Baptism of Christ. On the altar stands a High Gothic statue of St Catherine (c. 1430).

Three altars lie along the southern side of the nave: the **Altar of St Leopold** (1905), surrounded by a baldachin (1448) by Hans Puchsbaum, the **Altar of the Trinity**, adorned with a painting by Michelangelo Unterberger, and the **Altar of St Sebastian** (18th-century) that stands beside a double-rowed Baroque pew (1640).

> **Underground site**
> From the Stephansplatz underground station you can visit the underground remains of the **Virgil Chapel** (c. 1220), which stood on the Stephansplatz until 1781; the original site of the chapel is marked on the pavement. The chapel now houses an historic ceramics collection (open Tues–Sun 1.30–4.30pm).

DIOCESAN MUSEUM

North of the Dom on Stephansplatz is the site of the ★ **Dom- und Diözesanmuseum** (Cathedral and Diocesan Museum; No 6; open Tues–Sat 10am–5pm; tel: 51552 3689). As well as a fine crucified Christ by Lucas Cranach the elder (1537) and carving salvaged from the bombing of Stephansdom, the museum also contains the 14th-century portrait of Rudolf IV the Founder.

Walk through the arcade to the Wollzeile (No 2) to the entrance of the **Archbishop's Palace** ⓭. This Baroque building was constructed between 1638 and 1669 by Giovanni Coccapani (unfortunately there is no access to the public).

Portrait of Rudolf IV in the Diocesan Museum

2: Graben to Michaelerplatz

This route gives you two ways of getting from Graben, Vienna's central shopping street, to Michaelerplatz in front of the Hofburg.

In about 1220, during the extensions to the town under Duke Leopold VI, the former town moat surrounding the Roman camp was filled in and built upon. Subsequently becoming a market-place, during the reign of the Empress Maria Theresa, the street became the centre of Viennese city life, a role the ★ **Graben** continues to fulfil today. In 1804 Johann Martin Fischer sculpted the twin fountains, which are dedicated to two saints: St Leopold (southeast side) and St Joseph (north-west side). Beneath St Joseph's Fountain are some delightful Art Nouveau public conveniences, built in the early 1900s.

Below: Braun & Co.'s shopfront on Graben
Bottom: the Pestsäule at night

THE PLAGUE COLUMN

Between the fountains stands the ★ **Pestsäule** ⑭ (Plague Column). Emperor Leopold I had the column erected between 1682 and 1692 in fulfilment of a vow he had made during the terrible plague epidemic of 1679. The basic design was the work of Johann Fischer von Erlach, who took charge of the unfinished project in 1687 and sculpted the six reliefs surrounding the base (Creation, Plague,

Map
on pages
18–19

the Passover, the Last Supper, the Great Flood and Pentecost). Lodovico Burnacini designed the Cloud Obelisk, which was completed by Paul Strudel, with sculptures of allegorical figures of Faith vanquishing the Plague, angels bearing inscriptions, a likeness of the Emperor and the Holy Trinity.

PETERSKIRCHE AND KOHLMARKT

The first route leads down Graben, via St Peter's Church and Kohlmarkt to Michaelerplatz.

The foundation of ★★ **Peterskirche** ⑮ (St Peter's Church) in 792 (possibly on the site of a late-Roman church dating from the 4th century) is usually ascribed to Charlemagne, thus making it the second-oldest church in the city (after St Rupert's, *see page 55*). The present high Baroque building was begun by Gabriele Montani in 1702 and completed between 1703 and 1733, probably by Johann Lukas von Hildebrandt.

Shop fronts
Graben and Kohlmarkt have a number of 19th-century and Jugendstil shop fronts, as well as some more daring modernist designs. Of particular interest are Paolo Piva's reworkings of two of Adolf Loos' buildings. On Graben, he designed the extension to the Knize-shop (No 11), and on Kohlmarkt, the exterior and fittings for Schullin, tucked into the side of the Loos Haus. (Schullin used Hans Hollein to design their shopfront at 26 Graben.)

ST PETER'S INTERIOR

The interior is richly ornamented with stucco; the oval-shaped cupola opens up into a fresco depicting the *Assumption of the Virgin Mary* (1714) by Johann Michael Rottmayr. On the pillars supporting the dome can be seen the Evangelists and the

The Peterskirche dome frescoes

Fathers of the Church; they are the work of Johann Georg Schmidt (Schmidt of Vienna). The altarpieces (c. 1714) in the east side chapels depict *St Anthony* (Martino Altomonte), *St Francis of Sales* (Rottmayr) and *The Fall of the Angels* by JG Schmidt. Beside the latter is a painting of *St John Nepomuk Falling from the Bridge* (c. 1729), purportedly executed after sketches by Matthias Steindl. The high altar was created by Santino Bussi after a design by Bibiena. Above the tabernacle is a *Maria Immaculata* (1836) by Leopold Kuppelwieser; the altarpiece, by Martino Altomonte, depicts St Peter and St John healing a lame man. The Baroque pulpit was sculpted by Matthias Steindl in 1716. The altar painting (1712–14) represents the *Holy Family* by Martino Altomonte, a *Martyrdom of St Sebastian* by Anton Schoonjans and an *Execution of St Barbara* by FK Remp.

Star Attraction
● **Peterskirche**

Matthias Steindl's Baroque pulpit

KOHLMARKT

On the Kohlmarkt (formerly the city's Coal Market), as well as its many designer shops, is one of the most famous of Vienna's cafés, **Demel**. The 1880s gilded and mirrored interior is very elegant, and the cakes are some of the best in the city. At the bottom end of Kohlmarkt is Michaelerplatz (*see page 38*).

TO ALBERTINAPLATZ

The second way down to Michaelerplatz starts in the Dorotheergasse, named after a convent which once stood here, opposite the first fountain on Graben. At No 11 is the ★ **Jüdisches Museum der Stadt Wien ⓰** (Jewish Museum of the City of Vienna), which describes the often brutal Jewish experience of life in Vienna, and houses notable temporary exhibitions (open Sun–Fri 10am–6pm, Thurs 10am–8pm; tel: 535 0431; www.jmw.at). The museum also has a bookshop and a pleasant café.

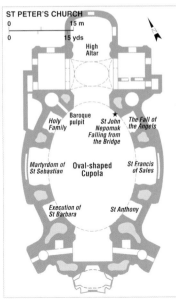

ST PETER'S CHURCH

0 ——— 15 m
0 ——— 15 yds

High Altar

Baroque pulpit

Holy Family

St John Nepomuk Falling from the Bridge

★ The Fall of the Angels

Martyrdom of St Sebastian

Oval-shaped Cupola

St Francis of Sales

Execution of St Barbara

St Anthony

Further down Dorotheergasse you come to the two **protestant churches** ⑰. The one on the right (1783–4) is classical in design and adheres to the Calvinist tradition. The Lutheran church on the left was designed by the court architect, Jacob Vivian, in 1582–3. The original Renaissance style of the interior has been preserved.

Statue of Providence on the Donner Fountain

DONNER FOUNTAIN

Walking down Plankengasse opposite leads to the Neuermarkt, the New Market, which was once the city's flour market. In the middle stands the famous ★ **Donner Fountain** ⑱, one of the finest and most artistically important in Vienna. The official name is the Providentia Fountain, but the local citizens always refer to it by the name of the sculptor who created it between 1737 and 1739, Georg Raphael Donner.

KAPUZINERKIRCHE

South, along Tegethoffstrasse, you come to the **Kapuzinerkirche** ⑲ (Church of the Capuchins). By the church, built from 1622 to 1632 and rebuilt in 1936 in accordance with the original plans, stands a statue of St Marco d'Aviano who, as a priest, accompanied the army sent to relieve the city of Vienna when it was besieged by the Turks in 1683. The altar in the north transept is adorned by a fine *Pietà* (1712) by Peter von Strudel.

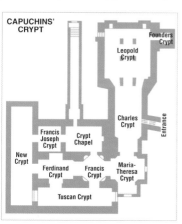

THE KAISERGRUFT

To the left of the church is the entrance to the ★★ **Kaisergruft** (Capuchins' Crypt, 1699; open daily 9.30am–4pm). With only two exceptions, the Holy Roman and Austrian emperors are buried here in elaborately tooled sarcophagi. The most important are: the Founders Crypt, with the sarcophagi of Emperor Matthew (1557–1619) and his consort Anne (1585–1618). In front lies the Leopold Crypt, with the monument to Leopold I (1640–1705). Balthasar Moll designed the fine Rococo sarcophagus of Charles VI (1685–1740) in the Charles Crypt; he was also responsible for the magnificent double sarcophagus made for Empress Maria Theresa (1717–80) and her consort, Emperor Francis of Lorraine (1708–65) in the Maria Theresa Crypt. In front stands the plain metal coffin of Emperor Joseph II (1741–90). The Francis Crypt has the monument by Peter Nobile to Emperor Francis II (1768–1806), who reigned as Emperor Francis I of Austria between 1804–35. In the Ferdinand Crypt is the sarcophagus of Emperor Ferdinand I of Austria (1793–1875). To the left is the Tuscan Crypt, with the remains of that branch of the imperial family.

In the New Crypt are the graves of Emperor Maximilian of Mexico (1832–67) and Napoleon's second wife, Marie-Louise (1791–1847). The Francis Joseph Crypt contains the sarcophagi of Francis Joseph I (1830–1916), Empress Elizabeth ('Sissi'; 1837–98), and Crown Prince Rudolph (1858–89). Their enduring popularity in Austria ensures that their tombs are still covered in flowers.

The last empress of Austria, Empress Zita, who died in 1989 (born 1892), was buried in the crypt chapel. There is also a memorial to her husband, Emperor Charles I (reigned 1916–18), who died in 1922 in Funchal, Madeira.

Star Attraction
● **Kaisergruft**

Fountain statues
The female figure in the middle of the Donner Fountain personifies Providence, with her all-foreseeing genius; the four figures on the edge of the basin represent four of the principal rivers which contributed to the creation of Austria: the Enns, the March, the Traun and the Ybbs. The original figures, which were cast in lead, can be seen in the Belvedere *(see page 63)*; they were replaced by copies in 1873.

The sarcophagi of Franz Joseph I and 'Sissi'

Map on pages 18–19

Below: The Warning Against Fascism and War
Below: Lobkowitz Palace door

THE ALBERTINA

At the bottom of Tegethoffstrasse is Albertinaplatz. The ★★★ **Albertina ㉑**, a palace which dates from 1781, houses the Graphic Collection founded by Duke Albert of Saxony-Teschen (tel: 534 830; www.albertina.at). With 60,000 drawings and 1 million sheets of etchings, engravings and lithographs it is the largest and most important collection of its kind in the world. The most valuable exhibits are works by Albrecht Dürer, Lucas Cranach, Leonardo da Vinci, Michelangelo, Raphael, Titian, Rubens and Rembrandt. The Neoclassical staterooms of the museum (which was closed from 1999 until spring 2003) have been fully restored, and a new hall for temporary exhibitions, a study building and state-of-the-art storage facilities have been built into the old city bastion behind the palace.

On the **Albertinaplatz** stands the composite *Warning against Fascism and War*, a memorial erected from 1988 to 1991 by Alfred Hrdlicka, in memory of the Anschluss of Austria with the Third Reich and the 'new beginning' in 1945. On the western side of the the square can be seen the **Albrechtsrampe ㉒**. Adorning the remaining section of the former Augustine Bastion are an equestrian statue (1898–9) of Archduke Albert, the work of Kaspar Zumbusch, and a Danube Fountain dating from 1869.

LOBKOWITZ PALACE

The **Lobkowitz Palace** ㉒ (open Tues–Sun 10am–5pm, Wed 10am–8pm; guided tours available, tel: 512 8800; www.theatermuseum.at), a patrician mansion erected in 1685 by Giovanni Pietro Tencala, acquired its magnificent Baroque doorway in 1716, made by Johann Bernard Fischer von Erlach. It was here that Beethoven's *Eroica* Symphony was heard for the first time in 1805.

The excellent ✶✶ **Österreichisches Theatermuseum** (Austrian Theatrical Museum) is housed within the palace. On the ground floor is a collection of models showing the development of European theatrical architecture, on the first floor – as well as the **Eroica Saal** – are a series of displays, including costumes, an 'orchestra pit', a puppet theatre and famous set models.

AUGUSTINERKIRCHE

Head down Augustinerstrasse to the ✶ **Augustinerkirche** ㉓ (Church of the Augustinians), founded in 1327 by Duke Frederick the Handsome as the court parish church; it was built between 1330 and 1339 to plans by Dietrich Ladtner von Pirn. The tower was a later addition (1652). The Baroque interior was removed in 1784 and the original Gothic character reinstated.

To the right of the entrance in the Josefsplatz lies the ✶ **marble memorial to Archduchess Marie Christine**, the favourite daughter of Empress Maria Theresa, designed from 1798 until 1805 by Antonio Canova. A masterpiece of the Empire period, the tomb recalls a burial pyramid. An allegorical figure of Virtue approaches the entrance, followed by Charity leading a blind man. Opposite the funeral procession, a spirit leaning on the back of a lion is holding a shield bearing the coat of arms of Saxony, the native kingdom of Marie Christine's consort, Prince Albert of Saxony-Teschen. The Archduchess herself can be seen on a carved medallion.

To the right of the choir is the entrance to the Gothic Chapel of St George (c. 1337), with the (empty) tomb of Emperor Leopold II (1790–2).

Star Attractions
● Albertina
● Österreichisches Theatermuseum

Royal remains
The room next door to the Gothic Chapel of St George is the *Herzgruft* of the Habsburg emperors. According to family tradition, the latter could only be buried after the heart and entrails had been removed from the body. The hearts of the Habsburgs, from Emperor Ferdinand II (died 1637) to Archduke Francis Charles (died 1878), are preserved here in small silver urns (open Mon–Fri 10am–noon; Wed 3–6pm; tel: 533 7099).

The Augustinerkirche tower

Map on pages 18–19

MICHAELERPLATZ

The end point of both routes is **Michaelerplatz**, an important crossroads as early as Roman times. Recent excavations in the centre of the square have revealed the remains of a 4th-century Roman house (fragments of its murals have been left in place), 1st to 5th century Roman walls, the 13th-century well cellar of a house and medieval drainage systems, as well as the remains of the old Burgtheater *(see page 82)*.

The Loos Haus

At the corner of Herrengasse and Kohlmarkt stands the ★★ **Loos Haus**. Adolf Loos provoked a scandal with the straight lines and unadorned facade of the building in 1910, even arousing the displeasure of Emperor Francis Joseph. But attitudes change and today his work is regarded as a masterpiece of modern architecture.

MICHAELERKIRCHE

The former parish church of the Austrian Emperors, ★★**Michaelerkirche** ㉔ (St Michael's Church) dates in part from 1221, although the building was extended during the 14th and 15th century. The tower is Gothic (1340–4), but its slender helm roof acquired its present appearance in 1590. Ferdinand von Hohenberg added the classical details to the facade, retaining nonetheless the Baroque porch (1724–5) by Antonio Beduzzi, with its lovely group of sculptures entitled *The Fall of the Angels*, by Lorenzo Mattielli. Against the outside of the south wall is a painted stone relief of *Christ on the Mount of Olives* dating from 1494.

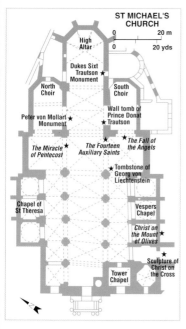

ST MICHAEL'S CHURCH

0 — 20 m
0 — 20 yds

High Altar

Dukes Sixt Trautson Monument ★

North Choir

South Choir

Peter von Mollart ★ Monument

Wall tomb of Prince Donat ★ Trautson

The Miracle ★ of Pentecost

The Fourteen ★ Auxiliary Saints

★ The Fall of the Angels

★ Tombstone of Georg von Liechtenstein

Chapel of St Theresa

Vespers Chapel

Christ on the Mount ★ *of Olives*

★ Sculpture of Christ on the Cross

Tower Chapel

The church is well worth a visit for its fine altar paintings and remarkable number of noblemen's tombs. Past the Baroque baptismal chapel is a larger-than-lifesize sandstone sculpture of Christ on the Cross dating from 1430. In the Tower Chapel are 13th-century Gothic frescoes of Saints Cosma, Thomas and Damian and a *Mass of St Gregory* (14th century). The altar of the magnificent Vespers Chapel contains a *Pietà* (c. 1430); the relief tombstone of Georg von Liechtenstein dates from 1548. The vast painting hanging above the north transept portrays *The Fall of the Angels*, completed in 1751 by Michael Unterberger. The south choir bay was donated in 1350 by the Ducal chef Stiborius Chrezzel in grateful thanks for his acquittal on a poisoning charge. Also dating from this period are the Gothic stone statues of St Catherine (left) and St Nicholas (right).

Star Attractions
● **Loos Haus**
● **Michaelerkirche**

ALTARPIECES

Tobias Pock was responsible for the altarpiece *The Fourteen Auxiliary Saints*, dating from 1643, adorning the altar in the Chapel of St John Nepomuk. Josef Emanuel Fischer von Erlach designed the wall tomb of Prince Donat Trautson in 1727; the monument (1663) to the two Dukes Sixt Trautson lies behind the choir screen. The ★ **high altar** is adorned with a portrait of the Madonna supported by angels (16th-century) from Iraklion (Crete); to one side are statues of the Evangelist (1781) by Johann Michael Fischer von Erlach. At the end of the choir there reoccurs the theme of the Fall of the Angels (18th-century, by Karl Georg Merville). The funeral monument to Peter von Mollart dates from 1576; the altar beside it is surmounted by a painting of *The Miracle of Pentecost* (c. 1643) by Tobias Pock. In the north side choir are two epitaphs by Georg von Herbenstein (1570) and Johann von Werdenberg (1643), as well as a memorial to the court poet, Metastasio, who died in 1782.

Below: The Fall of the Angels
Bottom: The Loos Haus

Map on pages 18–19

Below: statues of Hercules flank the Michaelertor
Bottom: the imperial eagle over the Michaelertor

3: The Hofburg

The enormous size and spendthrift pomp of the ★★★ **Hofburg** ㉕, the residence of the Habsburg family from the reign of Albert I (1283–1308) until the end of the Austro-Hungarian monarchy (1918), symbolises the power and wealth of the Austria of the past. Although the building itself was constructed over many centuries, from the Gothic age until the Historicist Ringstrasse era, the complex as a whole manifests a remarkably harmonious appearance. The beginning of World War I prevented the addition of a further wing on the site of what is now the Volksgarten. Had it been implemented, a unique 'Imperial forum' would have been created between the old wings and the Exhibition Palace beyond the Museumstrasse, encompassing both museum complexes.

THE MICHAELERTRAKT

The route begins at the Michaelerplatz *(see page 38)*. Dominating the square is the massive facade of the **Michaelertrakt**. This wing of the palace, started in 1735 by Josef Emanuel Fischer von Erlach, was not completed until 1893. The main entrance, the Michaelertor, arches over a passageway which for centuries had led from the city past the former ducal residence (Schweizerhof).

On each side are four statues of Hercules (end of the 19th century). Of particular note are the wall fountains adorning the facade: on the right, the *Mastery of the Land* designed in 1897 by Edmund Hellmer, and, on the left, the *Mastery of the Sea*, by Rudolf Weyr (1895).

Go under the vast domed archway and on the right you will find the entrance to the Imperial **Silberkammer** (Silver Collection) and the ★**Kaiserappartements** (the living quarters of Emperor Francis Joseph, Empress Elizabeth and Emperor Charles I), which were situated in the Imperial Chancellery wing, and the Amalienburg (open daily 9am–5pm, last ticket sales 4.30pm; guided tours in German: Silberkammer 11am and 3pm; Kaiserappartements 10am and 4pm; special tours by arrangement, tel: 533 7570).

THE RIDING SCHOOL

Leading off the Michaelerplatz, the narrow Reitschulgasse leads to the **Winterreitschule**, home of the famous Spanische Reitschule (Spanish Riding School; *see box*). The main building is the work of Josef Emanuel Fischer von Erlach. It was constructed between 1729 and 1735, and the huge parade hall is considered a masterpiece of Baroque architecture. A number of highly elaborate ceremonies were held here at the time of the Congress of Vienna.

Opposite lies the ★**Stallburg** (stables). The building was constructed in 1558 in the Renaissance style, on what was probably the site of the ducal palace erected in about 1220 by Leopold VI of Babenberg. In the arcaded courtyard stands a fine wrought iron well dating from 1558.

NATIONALBIBLIOTHEK

By the Winterreitschule is Josefsplatz, in the middle of which stands Franz Anton Zauner's equestrian statue (1795–1807) of Emperor Joseph II. Behind the statue is the main building of the ★★**Nationalbibliothek** (National Library), which contains around 2.2 million manuscripts and

Star Attractions
- Hofburg
- Nationalbibliothek

Classical equestrians
On the ground floor of the Stallburg are the stables of the world-famous Lipizzaner horses of the Spanish Riding School, the last in the world to retain the classical equestrian tradition. The stables are no longer open to the public, following an epidemic. However, visitors can see into six of the 68 stalls from behind a glass screen in the **Lipizzaner Museum** next door (open daily 9am–6pm). It is also possible to attend the performances and the morning training sessions in the Winterreitschule.

A Lipizzaner performs in the Winterreitschule

Map on pages 18–19

The Nationalbibliothek Baroque interior

printed books, maps, portraits, musical scores, papyrus documents and a globe museum. This building – the former Imperial Library – is one of the most important sites designed by Johann Bernhard Fischer von Erlach; it was constructed between 1723 and 1735 under the supervision of his son, Josef Emanuel. The central section is dominated by the flamboyant group *Minerva Driving her Chariot* (1725) by Lorenzo Mattielli.

Ascending the staircase (decorated with old gravestones), the visitor enters the **Prunksaal**, which occupies both upper storeys and which is the largest library room in Europe (open Mon–Sat 10am–4pm, Thurs 10am–7pm, Sun 10am–2pm). The ceiling frescoes (1730) by Daniel Gran depict the apotheosis of the library's founder, Emperor Charles VI. The painting in the oval dome portrays allegorical figures of the Sciences surrounded by patrons of the House of Habsburg; under the dome stand statues of Charles VI and 16 other Habsburg rulers (c. 1700, by Paul and Peter Strudel).

On the northeastern side of the square are two fine palaces. The earlier, Baroque Palais Palffy dates from 1575, while to the left is the Palais Pallavini (1783–4).

SCHWEIZERHOF

Leaving the Josefsplatz and crossing the Chapel Court (to the left lies the Gothic choir of the Imperial Chapel), the visitor enters the oldest part of the palace, the **Schweizerhof** (Swiss Court).

On the south side of the courtyard lies the entrance to the **Burgkapelle** (Castle Chapel), built in 1447 under Frederick III in place of an older (13th-century) building and rebuilt on several occasions between the 17th and 19th centuries. All that remains of the Gothic interior are 13 wooden statues by the columns, carved by Niclas Gerhaert van Leyden between 1470 and 1480, and, to the left of the side altar, a 15th-century statue of the Madonna (conducted tours mid-Jan–Jun and mid-Sept–mid-Dec, Mon–Thurs 11am–3pm, Fri 11am–1pm; Mass with the Vienna Boys' Choir; Sun 9.15am, Sept–Jun only, *see page 110*).

SCHATZKAMMER

Underneath the entrance to the chapel is the ★★★ **Schatzkammer** (the Secular and Ecclesiastical treasury; open Wed–Mon 10am–6pm). This, perhaps the most important national collection in the world, is divided into two sections: the Secular, and the Sacred or Liturgical Treasure.

THE SECULAR TREASURES

The first of the exhibits are **Die Österreische Erbhuldigung**, the insignia of the Archdukes of the Austrian territories. These are followed by **family insignia of the Habsburgs**, with, most significantly, the ★★ **crown of Emperor Rudolf II** (1602; from 1804 also the Austrian imperial crown), and the imperial orb and sceptre (c. 1612). Also here are the **Habsburg imperial insignia**, comprising the Imperial mantle, the Krönungsschwert (sword of state) and ceremonial jewels.

The displays that follow include the herald's mantle and stock of Lombardy-Venetia (1837–8), Napoleonic memorabilia from Napoleon's son and Archduke Maximilian (Emperor of Mexico 1863–7), and baptismal objects including golden christening items and baptismal robes.

Next come the priceless **Habsburg jewels**, including the Grand Cross of the Military Order of Maria Theresa (1765), a captured ★ diamond

Star Attractions
- Schatzkammer
- Crown of Rudolf II

Early Swiss
The Schweizerhof must have formed a part of the Babenburg castle of 1220; it was rebuilt following a fire in 1262 by King Ottokar II Premsyl of Bohemia and Rudolf I of Habsburg. The name first occurs in a document of 1279 and derives from the Swiss Guard battalion which was formerly quartered here. The arcades and the main gateway, the Swiss Gate, built between 1536 and 1553 are the most important of the few remaining examples of Renaissance architecture to be found in Vienna.

Coronation mantle from Palermo, 1133–4

Map on pages 18–19

sabre ('Hyacinth La Bella', Turkish, before 1683), and ★ Stephan Bocskay's crown (apostate Prince of Transylvania, Turkish, c. 1605). Beyond are the **Inalienable heirlooms**: a huge agate dish (Istanbul, 4th century), and Ainkhürn (tooth of a narwhal).

The Habsburgs, as the last sovereigns of the Holy Roman Empire (800–1806), retained the Imperial insignia and relics. The **Coronation robes** comprise nine imperial robes of state (mostly Sicilian, 12th century) and the mantle of Roger II, King of the Normans, with its Arabic motifs.

The Emperor's imperial dignity was symbolised by the ★★★ **Imperial Crown of the Holy Roman Empire** (962), ★ Imperial orb (c. 1200) and sceptre (14th-century), ★ Imperial cross (c. 1024), ★ Imperial sword (11th-century), ★ Coronation missal (pre-800), Charlemagne's sabre (10th-century), the ceremonial sword of Frederick II (pre-1220), and the Bursa of St Stephen (9th-century).

The **Burgundian Treasures** include mantles, swords (pre-1500) and the ceremonial chalice of the court. These are followed by **the Order of the Golden Fleece** (ceremonial objects, the ★ insignia chain and ★ ceremonial cross of the chivalrous order founded in 1429); and ★★ **the Paramental Treasure** (Communion objects of the Order of the Golden Fleece – altar hangings and liturgical vestments, Burgundian 1425–40 – including the 'most noble vestments in the world').

Below: gilded glass in the Schatzkammer
Bottom: the crown, orb and sceptre of the Holy Roman Empire

SACRED TREASURES

The valuable **Sacred treasures** comprise liturgical vestments for the Habsburg court services, magnificent liturgical objects and communion items (the Star Monstrance), and reliquaries (including nails from the Cross and particles of the Cross) dating from the 12th to 19th centuries.

The **Imperial relics**, part of the Holy Roman collections, are seven reliquaries including a splinter from Christ's crib, a tooth of St John the Baptist and pieces of Christ's tablecloth and loincloth from the Last Supper.

SCHWEIZERTOR TO HELDENPLATZ

The Schweizertor (Swiss Gate) leads into the busy square known as **In der Burg**. Surrounding the courtyard from right to left are:

Reichskanzleitrakt: the wing housing the imperial administration (until 1806) was designed by Johann Lukas von Hildebrandt and Josef Emanuel Fischer von Erlach between 1723 and 1730; the four sculptures *(The Labours of Hercules)* are the work of Lorenzo Mattielli who was active at the same time.

Amalienburg: the building, which was started under Emperor Maximilian II in the early-Baroque style, was finished in 1611 during the reign of Emperor Rudolf II by Pietro Ferrabosco and Antonio de Moys. It was named after Amalia of Brunswick, the consort of Emperor Joseph I. Empress Elizabeth, the consort of Emperor Francis Joseph I, also lived here.

Leopoldischertrakt: the building, constructed in 1660–6 under Emperor Leopold I by Domenico and Martin Carlone in accordance with a design by Philiberto Luchesi, serves today as the official residence of the president of Austria.

A passage leads from In der Burg to spacious **Heldenplatz** (Heroes Square), with its monuments (1860–5) by Anton Fernkorn. To the north is the memorial to Archduke Charles's victory over Napoleon I in 1809 at Aspern; to the south, that to the victor over the Turks in the 17th century, Prince Eugène of Savoy.

Star Attractions
- **Crown of the Holy Roman Empire**
- **Paramental Treasure**

Allegorical statues
The monument in the centre of the Schweizertor represents the Austrian Emperor Francis I (Francis II of the Holy Roman Empire) as a Roman emperor, surrounded by allegorical figures of Strength, Peace, Faith and Justice (1842–6, designed by Pompeo Marchesi).

The equestrian statue of Prince Eugène of Savoy

Map
on pages
18–19

THE NEUE BURG

Representative of the might of a great world power, the **Neue Burg** was built in 1881–1913 by Gottfried Semper and Karl von Hasenauer, on the instructions of Emperor Francis Joseph I.

Today the building houses the modern reading rooms of the National Library and four excellent ★★ **museums**. The huge **Museum für Völkerkunde** (Museum of Ethnology; open Wed–Mon 10am–4pm; tel: 534300; www.ethno-museum. ac.at) contains, among other items, three rare Aztec feather headdresses and superb Benin bronzes. The **Ephesos-Museum** holds items discovered by Austrian archaeologists in Turkey and Greece, while the **Hofjagd- und Rüstkammer** (Imperial Hunting Museum and Armoury) is the most important collection of weapons in Europe. The **Sammlung alter Musikinstrumente** (Collection of Historical Musical Instruments) has a strong collection of chordophones, and two beautiful silver trumpets. (All three museums open Wed–Mon 10am–6pm, tel: 52524; www.khm.at)

The Assembly Wing on the left of the Neue Berg is used today for holding balls and international congresses. Constructed in 1824, the **Burgtor** was transformed in 1933–4 into a memorial hall for those who fell during World War I. Since 1955 it has served as a Heroes' Monument, as Austria's Tomb of the Unknown Soldier.

The Burggarten
This park was laid out for the imperial family in the early 19th century. It has monuments to Francis Joseph I (1908, by Klimbusch) and Mozart (1896, by Viktor Tilgner). There is also the early 20th-century Jugendstil **Palmenhaus** (glass house) by Friedrich Ohmann. This contains a lovely café, and the Schmetterlinghaus, a butterfly garden (open Mon–Fri 10am–5pm, Sat–Sun 10am–6.30; Nov–Mar 10am–4pm).

*The Burggarten's Jugendstil
Palmenhaus*

4: The Chancellery to the Börse

This route takes you across the northern part of the Innere Stadt, from the centres of political power of the Hofburg and Federal Chancellery, to the centre of economic power of the Börse.

Star Attraction
●The Neue Burg museums

FEDERAL CHANCELLERY

Start in Ballhausplatz, in front of the **Bundeskanzleramt ㉖** (Federal Chancellery). The building was constructed between 1717 and 1719 by Johann Lukas von Hildebrandt to serve as a 'secret chancellery'.

The scene of many dramatic events, the Bundeskanzleramt saw the sessions of the Congress of Vienna that were held in 1814 and 1815; here, too, Chancellor Dollfuss of Austria was assassinated by National Socialists in 1934. Today, the building serves as the headquarters of the Austrian head of government and his foreign minister.

The Bundeskanzleramt entrance

IMPERIAL AND STATE ARCHIVES

Situated at the back of the building (Minoritenplatz 1) is the entrance to the **Haus-, Hof- und Staatarchiv ㉗** (Family, Court and State Archives; closed at present for renovation, visitors wishing to consult documents must apply at least 4 weeks in advance; tel: 53115 2500; www.oesta.gv.at). The collection, founded in 1740 under Maria Theresa, contains some 70,000 certificates, 3,000 manuscripts, 36,000 registered seals and 150,000 official books. The oldest manuscript in the collection is a document by Louis the Pious from 816, and the most valuable items are the counterfeit *Privilegium majis* (1359) by Rudolf IV the Founder and the 95 Theses by Martin Luther.

MINORITENKIRCHE

Although begun c. 1300 by French master builders, the unadorned **Minoritenkirche ㉘** (Church of the Minorities; open 8am–5pm) was not finished until 1447. In 1683 it lost the upper section of its

Map
on pages
18–19

Place name
Freyung, the name of the trapezium-shaped square, is probably linked to the Scottish Monastery's immunity from the jurisdiction of the local rulers and its right to grant asylum. According to legend, Johann Parricida, the murderer of Albert I, took refuge here in 1308. In the middle of the square stands the Austria Fountain, designed by Ludwig Schwanthaler in 1846. The statues of the four main rivers of Austro-Hungary (clockwise: the Elbe, the Vistula, the Danube and the Po) are crowned by an allegorical representation of Austria.

tower in an attack by the Turks. The Gothic main entrance (c. 1350) by Jacques de Paris has sculptures of the Madonna on the central pillar, reliefs of the saints surrounding the door and a crucifixion on the tympanum, which combine to make it one of the loveliest entrances in the whole of the city.

Inside are a ★ high altar painting of *The Virgin of the Snows* (1785) by Christoph Unterberger, paintings by Daniel Gran on the first and third altars on the right-hand side (pre-1750) and a mosaic copy based on Leonardo da Vinci's *The Last Supper* (1806–14, by Raffaeli).

Also worth studying are the former Palais Starhemberg (Minoritenplatz 5, now the Ministry of Education), which dominates one section of the square; and the Liechtenstein town palace next door (Minoritenplatz 4/Bankgasse 9), which was built between 1694 and 1706 by Domenico Martinelli and Gabriele de Gabrieli in the high Baroque style. Next door is the Palais Dietrichstein (1735) by Franz Hillebrand.

Continuing along the narrow Regierungsgasse, you will come to the Herrengasse, one of the city's main thoroughfares in Roman times.

LANDHAUS

The Minoritenkirche
Gothic doorway

On the left is the **Landhaus** ㉙ (Provincial Parliament of Lower Austria), constructed between

1837 and 1848, retaining elements of a previous building. The parliament has now moved, and the building is being renovated. The assembly chamber is decorated with frescoes (1710) by Antonio Beduzzi and it was in this place, on 12 October 1918, that the German-speaking members of the Imperial parliament decided to found the Republic of Austria. The Parliamentary Chapel (1516) is ascribed to Anton Pilgram.

Opposite the parliament building is the famous **Café Central**. At the end of the 19th century it was a favourite rendezvous of men of letters (Peter Altenberg, Franz Werfel, Karl Kraus *et al*), as well as the political revolutionary, Trotsky.

SCHOTTENKIRCHE

At the end of Herrengasse, on Freyung *(see box opposite)*, is the ★ **Schottenkirche** ⓾ (Scottish Church), built in 1155–1200 by Irish monks (Ireland was known at the time as 'Scotia maior'), after the Babenberg King Henry II Jasomirgott had summoned them to his country. Its present-day Baroque countenance is the result of rebuilding (1642–8) by members of the architect families Allio and Carlone; the interior (1882–93) was supervised by Heinrich von Ferstel. On the south front is a relief (1893) depicting the founding of the church, showing the king approving the building plans.

MEMORIALS

In the nave you will notice a number of fine memorials (17th–18th century); on the pillar in front of the third chapel on the left-hand side is the memorial plaque (c. 1725, by Josef Emanuel Fischer von Erlach) to Count Rüdiger von Starhemberg, who defended the city against the Turks in 1683. His tomb and that of King Henry II Jasomirgott lie in the crypt (entrance: Monumentenhalle, on the north side of the church). Of the altar paintings, those in the transept are worth mentioning: to the right a *Martyrdom of St Sebastian*, and to the left an *Assumption of the Blessed Virgin Mary*, both dated 1655 and both

Below: the tower and (bottom) interior of the Schottenkirche

Map
on pages
18–19

by Tobias Pock; on the triumphal arch is a *Crucifixion* (1654) and a *Farewell of St Peter and St Paul* (1652), by Joachim von Sandrart.

In the Schottenstift (Monastery of the Scots) adjoining the church (the building, designed by Josef Kornhäusl, dates from the 19th century) is a notable picture gallery (open Thurs–Sat 10am–5pm, Sun noon–5pm; tel: 5349 8600). The most important works are 19 Gothic paintings, originally by the high altar of the church, which show the earliest extant panoramas of Vienna. The gallery also has a collection of 17th- and 18th-century landscapes, portraits and religious paintings.

To the left stands the Ferstel Palace (1856–60, by H Ferstel), with a stone-covered facade.

Fiacre in front of the Kinsky Palace

KINSKY PALACE

The ★ **Kinsky Palace** ③, originally in the possession of the Daum family, was designed between 1713 and 1716 by Johann Lukas von Hildebrandt. It is one of the most characteristic patrician palaces in the city. Diagonally opposite stands the **Harrach Palace** ㉜. Built 1689–96, probably by Domenico Martinelli for Count Harrach, the palace was largely rebuilt in 1845 and restored with the aid of old etchings after suffering bomb damage during World War II. Since autumn 1999 it has housed an auction house.

HEIDENSCHUSS

Pass by the **Kunst Forum**, a display space that holds exhibitions of, mostly, modern and contemporary art (tel: 537 3311), to the short section of street between Freyung and Am Hof known as the **Heidenschuss** ㉝. The name derives from a house that once stood on the corner of the Strauchgasse and supposedly belonged to a family by the name of Haiden ('where the Haiden hangs out'). The legend tells of a baker's apprentice in 1529 whose attentiveness enabled the city to repulse the Turks, who had advanced to this point by the use of mines. The figure of a Turkish rider on the facade recalls the incident.

AM HOF

On the site of the present-day Bank Austria there once stood a castle built by Henry II Jasomirgott in 1138; it was the residence of the Dukes of Austria between 1156 and 1220. The square in front was used for jousting. Duke Leopold VI later gave the building to the Ducal Mint. Today, the ★ **Am Hof** ❸ (closed Mon) stands on the site of the chapel of the Mint. The church's Baroque facade (1662, by Carlo Carlone), added to the Gothic building of 1386, is a fine example of 17th-century architecture. On Easter Sunday 1782, Pope Pius VI, wishing to encourage Emperor Joseph II to adopt policies more favourable to the Church, blessed the people from the balcony. On 6 August 1806, from the same place, the dissolution of the Holy Roman Empire and the abdication of the imperial crown by Francis II was proclaimed.

In front of the church, the *Virgin's Column* (1664–7) by Carlo Carlone and Balthasar Herold recalls the Swedish threat during the Thirty Years War (1618–48): cherubs in armour fight against the evils of Plague, War, Hunger and Heresy.

> **Am Hof paintings**
> Of particular note inside the building are the wall paintings *The Flight into Egypt* and *Jesus in the Temple* (mid-17th century) by Joachim von Sandrart, in the second chapel on the right, as well as the ceiling fresco *St Francis of Regis* (mid-18th century) by Franz Anton Maulpertsch in the second chapel on the left, and the painting of St John Nepomuk (c. 1780) by Schmidt of Krems in the fourth chapel on the left. The high altar is adorned by the painting *The Virgin with the Nine Choirs of Angels* (1798) by Johann Georg Däringer.

THE TOWN ARSENAL

At the far end of the square stands the **Feuerwehr Zentrale** ❺. The building, built in 1530, originally served as a weapons store. Today it is the Fire

Am Hof church facade

Map on pages 18–19

Maria am Gestade

Brigade Headquarters and, further down, contains the **Feuerwehrmuseum** (Fire Brigade Museum; open Sun and public holidays 9am–noon, Mon–Fri by arrangement; tel: 531 99). The present Baroque facade was added in 1731 and 1732; the relief carvings are by Lorenzo Mattielli. Next door (No 9) there are guided tours of the Roman excavations (open Sat, Sun and public holidays 11am–1pm).

To the left of the church, walk through to the Schulhof, a small square surrounded by magnificent Baroque houses. At No 2 is the ★ **Uhrenmuseum** ㊱ (Clock Musem; open Tues–Sun 9am–4.30pm), housing a unique collection of some 21,200 exhibits, tracing the history of timekeeping.

Go back to Am Hof and walk along the narrow Drahtgasse to the Judenplatz, the centre of the Jewish ghetto in medieval Vienna. On one side stands the former **Böhmisce Hofkanzlei** ㊲ (Bohemian Chancellery), built from 1708 to 1714 to a design by Fischer von Erlach. It once served as the Imperial Ministry of Home Affairs. Today it houses the Austrian Constitutional and Administrative Courts of Justice.

In the centre of the square, surrounded by candles, is Rachel Whiteread's ★ **Holocaust Memorial** (2000). This cast of the interior space of a library refers to both 'the people of the book' and Israel's donation of books to libraries in memory of victims of the Holocaust.

THE OLD TOWN HALL

The ★ **Altes Rathaus** ㊳ (Old Town Hall) was a gift to the city in 1316 from Duke Frederick the Handsome. Rebuilt several times during the Baroque era, it served as Town Hall until 1883. In the courtyard, on the left-hand wall, is the Andromeda Fountain (1741) by Georg Raphael Donner. Cast in lead, it portrays Perseus freeing Andromeda from the dragon. From the courtyard, a passage on the right leads to **Salvatorkapelle** ㊴. Founded in around 1290, the building acquired much of its present appearance in 1360–1. Of note is the Renaissance portal (Salvatorgasse 5), with shields decorating the doorway and busts of Christ and the Virgin.

Until Vienna became a bishopric in 1469, the town lay under the jurisdiction of the Bishop of Passau, whose representatives lived in the Passauer Hof; they had ★★ **Maria am Gestade** ⑩ (Our Lady of the River Bank) built on a steep bank overlooking the main branch of the Danube, on the street known today as Salzgries. The church is mentioned for the first time in 1158.

Star Attraction
● Maria am Gestade

ROMAN TEMPLE

It is likely that a Roman temple dedicated to the goddess of fertility originally stood on this site, next to the military camp of Vindobona. The north wall of today's church stands on the foundations of the Roman fortifications. Between 1394 and 1414 Michael Chnab added the nave to the existing choir, which had been rebuilt from 1330 to 1357 following a fire in 1252. Between the two sections is a septagonal tower with a pierced dome that is one of the finest examples of Gothic art.

Inside, there is an Angel of the Annunciation (1380) on the sixth pillar on the left. In one of the side chapels stands a Renaissance altar (1520) with carvings of the Virgin, St John the Baptist and St Nicholas. The choir windows contain Gothic stained-glass panels. Of note amongst the rest of the interior (19th-century) is the sarcophagus of St Clement Hofbauer (1751–1820) in the choir.

The Börse
North of Judenplatz, at the end of Wipplingerstrasse, is the Börse ⑪, Vienna's stock exchange (unfortunately closed to visitors; tel: 531 650). The building, remarkable for its brick-red facade, was constructed between 1871 and 1877 by the Danish architect Theophil Hansen. It has been the headquarters of the Vienna stock exchange ever since. In 1956, a fire destroyed parts of the building including the securities hall. Following restoration work, the securities section was moved to another part of the building.

Theophil Hansen's Borse

Map
on pages
18–19

5: Hoher Markt to Fleischmarkt

This route through a labyrinth of old alleys gives an impression of life in Old Vienna. The oldest square in the city is the **Hoher Markt ㊷**; until the 12th century, it also marked its centre. The Roman commandant had his headquarters here, as can be seen from the excavations of the Roman officers' quarters of the X Legion (access: No 3; open Tues–Sun 9am–12.15pm and 1pm–4.30pm).

ANKERUHR

Spanning the alley know as Bauernmarkt is an archway bearing the **Ankeruhr ㊸**. This jacquemart clock, constructed from 1911 to 1917, presents every hour a figure from Austrian history; at noon, all the characters appear in procession and usually draw a crowd. (There is an explanation of all the different figures on a plaque on the left-hand side beneath the arch.)

Passing along the narrow Judengasse you will reach Seitenstettengasse. In the premises of the Israeli Cultural Association (No 4) is the main Synagogue built in 1825–6. Daily tours describe the important role played by the Jews of Vienna in the intellectual and cultural development of Europe (11.30am and 3pm; bring your passport for the security check; tel: 531 040).

👁 Square fountain
In the middle of Hoher Markt stands the high Baroque Fountain of the Virgin's Wedding, built by Josef Emanuel Fischer von Erlach between 1729 and 1732 from plans drawn up by his father. The main sculpture (by Antonio Corradini) represents the marriage of the Virgin Mary to Joseph.

The Art Nouveau Ankeruhr

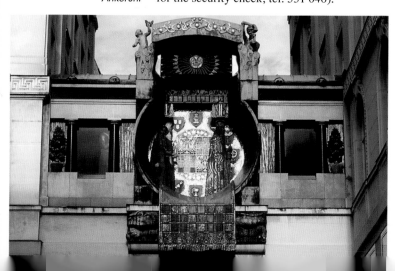

RUPRECHTSKIRCHE

★★ **Ruprechtskirche** ❹ (St Rupert's Church; open Mon–Fri 10am–1pm) was founded in 740, which makes it the oldest church in the city. The nave of the present Romanesque building and the lower section of the tower date from the 11th century. The central window in the choir contains the oldest example of stained glass in the city, a Crucifixion which dates from the end of the 13th century.

Turning back towards the Hoher Markt, cross Rotenturmstrasse and take Bäckerstrasse on the right by Lugeck Platz (note the Gutenberg Monument, 1902). The houses here have survived almost unchanged since the 17th and 18th centuries. In some cases, the facades hide buildings of even greater antiquity. No 7 has a pretty courtyard with Renaissance arcades (16th century). No 12 (15th and 16th centuries) is decorated with a cow playing a board game.

DR IGNAZ-SEIPEL-PLATZ

On Dr Ignaz-Seipel-Platz, which has hardly changed its appearance over the past two hundred years, stands the **Alte Universität** ❺ (Old University). Between 1623 and 1627 the building was made available for lectures, following Emperor Ferdinand II's decree placing the order in charge of the running of the university, founded in 1365.

From 1753 to 1854 the academic gatherings were held in the Aula across the road, today occupied by the **Akademie der Wissenschaften** ❻ (Academy of Science; open Mon–Fri 9am–5pm except when ceremonies are taking place; ask for details at the reception desk). The Rococo building, with its elaborate corner pavilions and niches for fountains, was erected in 1753 under the direction of Jean Nicolas Jadot de Ville-Issey. Of note are the ceiling paintings in the richly decorated first-floor hall (allegories of the four faculties), which are the work of Gregorio Guglielmi and date from 1755.

At the far end of the square is the ★★ **Jesuitenkirche** ❼, the old university church. The early-Baroque facade of the church, built from 1627

Star Attractions
● **Ruprechtskirche**
● **Jesuitenkirche**

Ruprechtskirche tower

Map
on pages
18–19

to 1632, is decorated with sculptured figures in niches. The top row (17th century) includes (from right to left) Saints Barbara, Leopold, Joseph and Catherine (the patroness of knowledge); the lower row depicts Jesuit saints: Francis Xavier (right) and Ignatius Loyola (left). The latter statues were carved by Andrea Pozzo, who also redesigned the interior from 1703 until 1705. Here, Pozzo attempted to make the nave the dominant feature with extensive gilding and striking spiral granite columns. The interior has been beautifully restored and particularly noteworthy are Pozzo's ceiling frescoes, with a *trompe l'oeil* dome and the Assumption of the Virgin adorning the high altar. It is also possible to see the wood-lined sacristy (1631–1720). The church has changing displays of contemporary art dotted around the nave.

Local legend
The name of the Basilisken-haus is derived from a stone in the form of a hen (its beak and comb were added to the stone later), which was found in 1212 in the well belonging to the house and which now adorns the facade. A Viennese legend tells of a monster which supposedly poisoned the well. A baker's apprentice climbed down and held a mirror in front of the creature, whereupon the poor thing was overcome with fear at its own ugliness and instantly turned to stone.

BASILISK HOUSE

Also a part of the university was the house at No 19 Sonnenfelsgasse (formerly the Pedell House, the *domus universitatis*), which has a wrought-iron balcony (1730). The Hildebrandt House (No 3; 1721) has a fine Baroque facade. Between the two houses is the entrance to Schönlaterngasse, one of the prettiest corners of Vienna. Here is the **Basiliskenhaus** ㊽, renovated during the 17th

The Jesuitenkirche nave century (*see box*).

HEILIGENKREUZERHOF

First mentioned in 1201, **Heiligenkreuzerhof** ⑭ the Viennese trading *dépendance* of Heiligenkreuz abbey *(see page 100)*, was laid out in its present form in 1659–76. The garden wall, with its sculptures from the atelier of Giovanni Giuliani (removed for restoration), dates from 1729. The Chapel of St Bernhard (1660, renovated 1730–80) looks unassuming from the outside, but contains ceiling frescoes by Antonio Tassi and an impressive high altar painting (*Manifestation of the Virgin*, 1730) by Martino Altomonte, next to which are statues of Saints Leopold and Florian (c. 1732) by Giovanni Giuliani.

The Byzantine tower of the Griechenkirche

Continuing along Schönlaterngasse, you reach Postgasse; on the right stands the ★ **Dominikanerkirche** ⑳. Duke Leopold the Glorious summoned the Dominicans to Vienna in 1226. Shortly afterwards work was begun on the construction of a Gothic church, but it soon collapsed. The present building, constructed 1631–4 by Jakob Spatz, Cipriano Biasino and Antonio Canevale, reveals the influence of Roman Baroque.

The interior has frescoes depicting the Life of the Virgin by Matthias Rauchmiller (the nave) and Franz Geyling (the dome). In the south transept is an *Adoration of the Shepherds* (1674) by Johann Spillenberger, and in the north transept a *St Dominic* (1717) by Tobias Pock. On the high altar is a picture of the Virgin (1839) by Leopold Kupelwieser.

GRIECHENKIRCHE

On the Fleischmarkt is the **Griechenkirche** ㉑ (Greek Church) with its ornate iconostasis. The original building (1782) acquired a Byzantine-style tiled facade in 1858, designed by Theophil Hansen. Also on Fleischmarkt is the stylishly revamped **Hauptpost** (post office; No 1) in a restored 18th-century Benedictine monastery.

In the nearby **Griechenbeisl Inn**, in the mid-17th century, Augustin Mitte is said to have first sung his famous *O, du lieber Augustin* in the bar. Famous guests such as Beethoven, Franz Grillparzer and Johann Strauss have left their signatures on one of the ceilings.

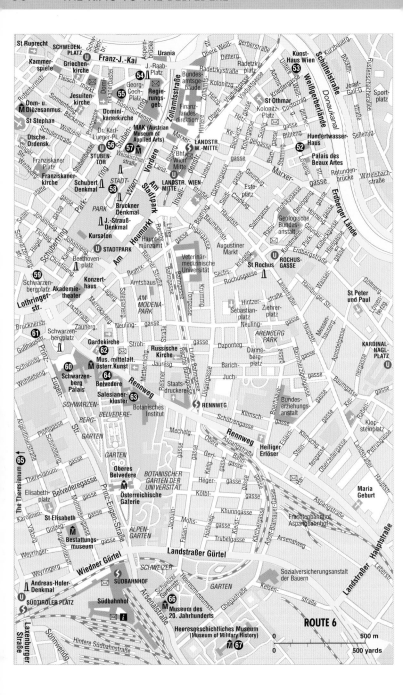

ROUTE 6

6: The Ring to the Belvedere

This route leads outside the limits of the medieval city north through a district built up during the 19th century, and then away from the Ringstrasse in a southeasterly direction. *(See map opposite.)*

HUNDERTWASSER HIGHLIGHTS

Start at the colourful ★★ **Hundertwasserhaus** ❷ (intersection of Löwengasse and Kegelgasse, signposted from Rochusgasse U-Bahn station; www.hundertwasserhaus.at). Rounded corners, varied window shapes, landscaped terraces with trees, stucco figures, pillars and golden cupolas adorn the remarkable council flats (1983–5) designed by Friedensreich Hundertwasser. Out of consideration for the residents, the building is not open to the public. Next door stands the **Village**, a little arcade of shops also designed by Hundertwasser (1990–1), with a cheerful interior design. The toilets here are also well worth seeing.

Walk up Untere Weissgerberstrasse to No13, ★ **KunstHaus Wien** ❸ (open daily 10am–7pm; www.kunsthauswien.com). Hundertwasser redesigned the facade of the building in which the Thonet Company once manufactured its ground-breaking bentwood furniture, creating a space for the artist's paintings, graphic works, tapestries and models. There is a museum shop, a lovely café, and there are changing exhibitions on the third floor.

RADETZKY, WAGNER AND LUEGER

At the beginning of the Stubenring is the **monument** ❹ to Josef Count Radetzky, a popular Austrian field-marshal during the 19th century. From here it is a short walk to Georg-Coch-Platz and the ★★ **Postsparkasse** ❺ (Post Office Savings Bank). Built 1904–6 and designed by Otto Wagner, the building is one of the finest examples of Art Nouveau architecture in Vienna. The Secessionist style is recognisable in the 'nailed' technique employed for the marble cladding and the design of the ledge.

Star Attractions
● Hundertwasserhaus
● Postsparkasse

Colourful architect
The artist and architect Friedensreich Hundertwasser (1928–2000) was inspired by the idea of building in harmony with human and natural requirements. He is responsible for several colourful and idiosyncratic buildings across Vienna. Not everyone is convinced, however, by his creations. One critic wrote of him: '[his] remedial suggestions... are limited to the surface, but presented with all the fervour of a 19th-century quack flogging his bottles of coloured horsepiss as a miracle cure for all diseases'.

A KunstHaus detail

Below: Otto Wagner's
Postsparkasse
Bottom: the Stoclet Frieze by
Gustav Klimt in MAK

Stubenring leads to **Dr Karl-Lueger-Platz** 🛈. Dominating the centre is the memorial erected in 1927 to the popular mayor of Vienna, Dr Karl Lueger (1897–1910). His period of office was closely linked with the development of Vienna as a modern metropolis.

MAK

★★★ **MAK** 🛈 (Austrian Museum of Applied Arts) is now one of the most exciting museums in the city (open Tues 10am–midnight, Wed–Sun 10am– 6pm; tel: 7113 6298; www.mak.at). Built by Heinrich von Ferstel (1868–71) as an unfaced brick building with *sgraffito* painting, it has been completely renovated under director Peter Noever, and a modern extension built on the back.

The concept behind the museum's makeover was to trust the curating of each section of the museum to a different contemporary artist. The result is a widely varying take on different historical periods and their artefacts. Divided by historical period, from Romanesque, Gothic and Renaissance to 20th-century design and architecture, the displays help you re-examine familiar objects (e.g. chairs, ceramics and carpets) by placing them in a non-traditional museum environment.

The basement store has been opened to the public as a 'study collection', while the modern glass extension holds temporary exhibitions. There is also a great café/restaurant designed by Hermann Czech.

Particularly noteworthy are the open displays of Buddha statues in the basement, the collection of Baroque and Rococo glass and exquisite lace (curated by Franz Graf and Angela Völker), and the display of, largely Thornet, bentwood chairs shown in silhouette (curated by Barbara Bloom and Christian Witt-Dörring). Of great importance is the museum's collection of Wiener Werkstätte pieces (1903–32), including the factory's archive (curated by Heimo Zobernig and Elizabeth Schmuttermeier).

The facade of the Academy of Applied Arts next door (by the entrance to the café) has a mosaic picture (1873, by Salviati) of Pallas Athene.

STADTPARK AND SCHWARTZENBERG

In front of the MAK is the **Stadtpark ❸**. A remnant of the *glacis* (open defensive land around the city), the park was laid out along the Ringstrasse and the Vienna River in 1858–62, following plans by the landscape painter Josef Selleny. It is one of the most attractive parks in the city and also the most fashionable. Crossing the Beethovenplatz, dominated by a memorial (1880) to the composer, you will pass the Konzerthaus (1912–13) before arriving at the **Schwarzenbergplatz ❺**.

Behind the monument (1946) to the fallen Soviet troops, erected by the army of occupation of the time, is the **Schwarzenberg Palace ❻**. Nowadays the building, constructed between 1697 and 1714 to plans by Johann Lukas von Hildebrandt and with an interior designed from 1720 to 1730 by Johann Bernhard Fischer von Erlach, is partly a hotel and restaurant. The idyllic Schwarzenberg Gardens behind, with the *Abduction* group (18th-century) by Lorenzo Mattielli, are usually closed to the public.

Diagonally opposite stands the **French Embassy ❻**. Built from 1906 to 1909 to a design by GP Chédune, the embassy was originally intended for Istanbul. There was confusion when the plans were sent off, however, and the building planned for the Bhosphorus was built here and the Viennese one built in Istanbul.

Star Attraction
● MAK

> **Municipal art**
> The Stadtpark is famous for its many monuments: Mayor Andreas Zelinka by Franz Püringer (1877); Franz Schubert by Karl Kundmann (1872); the portraitist Amerling by Johannes Benk (1902); the painter Hans Makart and composer Anton Bruckner by Viktor Tilgner (1898–99); also the fountain group *The Liberation of the Spring* by Josef Heu (1903) and the *Danube Woman* fountain by Hans Gasser (1865). The most famous monument is the Johann Strauss Memorial, by Edmund Heller (1923). Waltz concerts are held from Easter to October (daily 4pm and 8pm) in the Assembly Rooms.

The French Embassy and Karleskirche from Schwarzenbergplatz

Map on page 58

THE GUARD CHAPEL

From Schwarzenbergplatz, follow Rennweg, a mule track in Roman times and the site of races during the 14th century. To the left lies the **Gardekirche** ⑫ (Guard Church; 1755–63), commissioned by Maria Theresa for her Polish bodyguard. The fine Rococo interior is decorated in white and gold. Above the Classical high altar is a *Crucifixion* (18th-century) by Peter Strudel.

On the right-hand side of Rennweg is the **Salesianerkloster** ⑬. The building was donated by Amalia of Brunswick on 13 May 1717, the day on which her granddaughter Maria Theresa was born. The design, executed by Donato Felice d'Allio, was completed by 1730 and is thought to be by Johann Bernhard Fischer von Erlach. The dome is decorated with a fresco (1727) of *The Assumption of the Virgin Mary* by Giovanni Antonio Pellegrini; the same artist also painted the *Handing over of the Keys* on the first altar on the left. The high altar painting of *The Visitation of Mary* is by Antonio Belucci.

Schwarzenberg view

In Schwarzenbergplatz, you will see in the middle of the square the equestrian statue (1864–7) by Ernst Julius Hähnel of Prince Karl von Schwarzenberg, the leader of the Austrian, Prussian and Russian armies against Napoleon I in the Battle of Leipzig (1813). At the south end of the square stands an impressive fountain (1873) which is illuminated at night during the summer months.

The dome of the Salesianerkloster

THE BELVEDERE

Next to the church lies one of the most important sights in Vienna: the ★★★ **Belvedere** ⑭ (www.belvedere.at). The high-Baroque summer palace of Prince Eugène of Savoy, who commanded the armies of Austria under three emperors, was Johann Lukas von Hildebrandt's greatest masterpiece in Vienna. Today the Belvedere houses three highly recommended museums.

The living quarters were in the **Unteres** (lower) **Belvedere**. Built from 1714 to 1716, the palace contains the two-storey Marble Hall with magnificent decorations (stucco reliefs and statues of trophies and Turkish prisoners). The ceiling fresco was painted by Martino Altomonte in 1716. It refers to Prince Eugène's victory at Peterwardein in 1714 and shows Apollo driving the chariot of the sun; underneath are the nine muses and, to the right, a portrait of the general. In the prince's sleeping quarters next door, the fresco by Altomonte depicts Apollo and Daphne and Luna and Endymion.

BAROQUE AND MEDIEVAL ART

Today the Lower Belvedere houses the ★★ **Barock-museum** (Baroque Museum; open Tues–Sun 9am–6pm; winter closes 5pm), a fine collection of Austrian Baroque painting and sculpture, including works by Franz Anton Maulbertsch (Rooms 18 and 19; 1724–96), Daniel Gran (Room 20; 1694–1757) and Peter Strudel (Room 4; 1660–1714). However, one of the most striking paintings is Jacques Louis David's Neoclassical *Napoleon on the St Bernard Pass* (Room 11; 1801).

Other highlights include: the original sculptures for the Donner Fountain *(see pages 34–5)*, housed in the Marble Hall; and Room 14 (Hall of the Grotesques), given over to the extraordinary grimacing busts by the sculptor Franz Xavier Messerschmidt. The furthest room (16) is the highly ornate Rococo gilt and mirrored Golden Cabinet, in the centre of which is Balthasar Permoser's statue *The Apotheosis of Prince Eugène*.

Adjoining the Lower Belvedere is the former **Orangery**, housing the ★★ **Museum Mittelaltericher Kunst** (Museum of Art of the Middle Ages; timings as above). This covers art of the Romanesque and late Gothic periods. Particularly impressive are *The Crucifixion* by Conrad Laib (1449), *The Mystical Marriage of St Catherine of Alexandria* by the Master of Heiligenkreuz (1380–90), and a series of works by Michael Pacher.

Star Attraction
● Belvedere and Museums

Below: Belvedere garden statues
Bottom: an Apotheosis by Franz Anton Maulbertsch

Map
on page
58

THE OBERES BELVEDERE

South of Unteres Belvedere lies the magnificent **Belvedere Park** (open 6.30am–5.30pm). It was laid out between 1700 and 1725 in the Classical French style to a design by Dominique Girard and decorated with fountains, pools, little waterfalls and avenues bordered by trimmed hedges. Near the Landstrasser Gürtel is an Alpine Garden, containing many rare species of alpine plants.

At the end of the terrace lies the **Oberes** (upper) **Belvedere** (1721–3), generally regarded as Johann Lukas von Hildebrandt's greatest masterpiece. Beside the Courtyard of Honour (alongside Landstrasser Gürtel), the attractive proportions of the facade are emphasised by a large pool.

The interior of the Garden Palace was designed by Claude le Fort du Plessy, whilst the stucco work was undertaken by Santino Bussi. The ceiling fresco *Apollo and Aurora* (The Victory of Light over Darkness) in the Garden Room, to the right of the entrance hall, is by Carlo Carlone. On 15 May 1955, the treaty returning Austria's independence and sovereignty was signed in the central hall on the upper floor, which has walls clad in red marble.

The ceiling fresco, the *Allegory of Fame*, is by Carlo Carlone, who was also responsible for the dome fresco *God the Father with the Holy Ghost* (1723) in the palace chapel. The altar there boasts a notable *Resurrection* by Francesco Solimena.

Diplomatic palace
The Theresianum ⑤ (Favoritenstrasse 15) lies to the west of the Belvedere. The former summer residence of the imperial family was built between 1687 and 1690 to a design by Lodovico Burnacini. Empress Maria Theresa had the palace converted into a college for young noblemen in 1746. Since 1966 the building has housed the Austrian College of Diplomacy.

The Oberes Belvedere facade

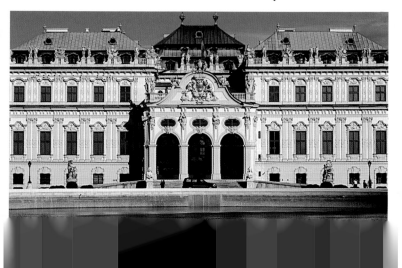

19TH- AND 20TH-CENTURY ART

The Oberes Belvedere houses the ★★★ **Österre-ichische Galerie** (Austrian Gallery; open Tues–Sun 9am–6pm; winter closes 5pm), a stunning collection of 19th and 20th century painting. The 3rd floor is devoted to Biedermeier, Neoclassical and Romantic works, the 2nd floor to art around 1900; temporary exhibitions are held on the ground floor.

Of the Neoclassical works, the portraits by Angelica Kaufmann are particularly fine (Room 5; *Countess Meerfeld*, 1790; Room 9; *Lord John Simpson*, 1773). Romanticism is well represented with two canvases by Casper David Friedrich (Room 9), *Rocky Landscape in the Elbsandsteingebirge* (1822–3), and *Seashore in the Mist* (1807). Perhaps the most famous works are on the 2nd floor, notably those by Gustav Klimt (Room 23), *The Kiss* (1907–8), the portrait of *Adele Bloch-Bauer* (1907) and *Apple Tree* (1912). Two other major Viennese artists represented are Oskar Kokoschka (Room 27), with his *Still Life with Dead Mutton* (1910), and Egon Schiele (Room 28), with *The Family* (1918). There are also some superb French Impressionist canvases (Room 16), including Renoir's *After the Bath* (1876) and *Bather with Loose Blond Hair* (1903), and Monet's *Anglers on the Seine at Poissy* (1882) and *Pathway in the Garden at Giverny* (1902).

ON FROM THE BELVEDERE

Close to the Belvedere are two other museums of interest (use the exit on Prinz-Eugene-Strasse). The **Museum des 20. Jahrhunderts** 🜶 (Museum of the 20th Century; open Tues–Sun 10am–6pm), previously the Austrian Pavilion at the World Exhibition in Brussels in 1958, houses changing art exhibitions. The neo-Gothic and Oriental **Heeresgeschichtliches Museum** 🜷 (Museum of Military History; open Sat–Thurs 9am–5pm) was commissioned by Emperor Francis Joseph and built by Theophil Hansen and Ludwig Förster between 1849 and 1856. It traces the history of the Austrian army from the Thirty Years' War (1618–48) to the outbreak of World War I.

Star Attraction
● **Österreichische Galerie**

Caspar David Friedrich's Rocky Landscape in the Elbsandsteingebirge

Map below

The portrait of Emilie Flöge by Klimt

7: Karlsplatz to Schillerplatz

From Schwarzenbergplatz *(see page 61)*, the Lothringerstrasse leads to the nearby Karlsplatz. Here is the ★★**Museum der Stadt Wien** ⑱ (Museum of Vienna; open Tues–Sun 9am–6pm; www.museum.vienna.at). The ground floor has Roman finds; frescoes, sculptures and some wonderful Gothic stained glass from Stephensdom, rescued after the choir was destroyed during World War II; and items from the Ottoman siege of Vienna in 1683. There are also some extraordinary heraldic devices. Of particular interest are the reconstructed former apartments of the writer Franz Grillparzer and the architect Adolf Loos.

The museum also has a significant collection of late-19th and early-20th century Viennese art, including Gustav Klimt's *Love* (1895) and portrait of *Emilie Flöge* (1902), Gerstl's portrait of *Arnold Schoenberg* (1905–6) and Franz Barwig's sculpture of a *Sitting Bear* (1905), as well as some beautiful 19th to early 20th-century costumes.

THE FRIENDS OF MUSIC

Opposite is the magnificent neo-Renaissance **Musikvereingebäude** ⑲ (Society of the Friends of Music). Constructed in 1867 to a design by Theophil Hansen, it is home to the Vienna Philharmonic Orchestra *(see page 108)*. The ceiling paintings *Apollo and the Nine Muses* (1911) are by August Eisenmenger.

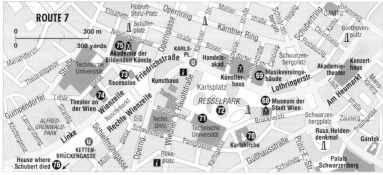

Beside the Academy of Music lies the ★ **Künstlerhaus** (1868), which houses art exhibitions (open Fri–Wed 10am–6pm, Thur 10am–9pm; www.k-haus.at). In front stand two ★ **Art Nouveau U-Bahn pavilions** built from 1899 to 1901 by Otto Wagner; one is now an exhibition space (open Tues–Sun 10am–6pm; closed 1 Nov–31 Mar), while the other is a café.

Star Attractions
● **Museum der Stadt Wien**
● **Karlskirche**

KARLSKIRCHE

Dominating Karlsplatz is the high-Baroque ★★ **Karlskirche 70**. When the city was devastated by an epidemic of plague in 1713, Emperor Charles VI vowed to build a church to the patron saint of plagues, St Carlo Borromeo. Johann Bernhard Fischer von Erlach began the construction in 1716; it was completed in 1737 under his son, Josef Emanuel. Fischer von Erlach's sketches show the influence of his apprenticeship in Rome. Today the massive dome (72m/236ft) makes the church the most important sacred building in Vienna after St Stephen's Cathedral. The pillared portico has a relief by Giovanni Stanetti in the tympanum, representing the vanquishing of the plague. Above the gable can be seen, from left to right, statues of Charles, Religion, Mercy, Repentance and Piety, all by Lorenzo Mattielli; in front of the portico are two statues of angels, one bearing the Cross, the other a Cross and a brazen serpent, symbols of the Old and New Testaments. On the triumphal pillars are bas-reliefs (1724–30, Johann Christoph Mader) of scenes from the life of St Carlo Borromeo.

The Karlskirche

THE DOME FRESCOES

Some of the most important Baroque artists of the time contributed to the interior decorations. Of particular interest are the dome frescoes, which were completed by Michael Rottmayr between 1725 and 1730; they represent *St Carlo*

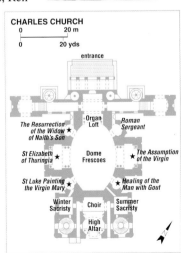

CHARLES CHURCH

0   20 m
0   20 yds

entrance

Organ Loft

Roman Sergeant

The Resurrection of the Widow ★ of Naith's Son

St Elizabeth ★ of Thuringia

Dome Frescoes

★ *The Assumption of the Virgin*

St Luke Painting ★ the Virgin Mary

★ *Healing of the Man with Gout*

Winter Sacristy

Choir

Summer Sacristy

High Altar

Map
on page
66

Karlskirche altars

The altar panels in the side chapels to the right depict *The Resurrection of the Widow of Nain's Son* (1731) by Martino Altomonte, a portrait of *St Elizabeth of Thuringia* (1736–7) by Daniel Gran, and *St Luke Painting the Virgin Mary* by Jakob van Schuppen. The high altar is of *St Carlo Borromeo in Glory* (1730), the work of the Prague sculptor Ferdinand Brokoff, based on designs by Johann Bernhard Fischer von Erlach. The altar paintings in the left side chapels portray the *Healing of the Man with Gout* by Antonio Pellegrini (1730), the *Assumption of the Virgin Mary* (1730) by Sebastiano Ricci and a *Roman Sergeant*, by Daniel Gran (1736).

The Secession's golden crown of bay leaves

in Glory flanked by groups depicting the three heavenly virtues of Faith, Hope and Love. To the left under the group portraying Faith are Luther and an angel; the angel is holding a torch with which he is burning Luther's Bible.

The fresco above the magnificent organ loft represents St Cecilia, the patron saint of music (c. 1730, by Rottmayr). To the left of the choir lies the summer sacristy; to the right is the winter sacristy; the latter contains the cardinal's hat of St Carlo Borromeo (northern Italian, 16th-century).

To the right of the church stands the **Technische Universität ⓐ** (Technical University). The main building, Classical in style, was constructed in 1816 and 1818 in accordance with plans drawn up by architects of the Imperial Ministry of Buildings. It is decorated with sculptures by Josef Klieber.

RESSELPARK

Stretching out from Karlskirche and the University is **Resselpark ⓑ**. As well as a memorial to the composer Johannes Brahms (1908, by Rudolf Weyr), the gardens contain memorials to a number of Austrian inventors: Josef Ressel, inventor of the ship's propeller (1862, by Anton Fernkorn), Josef Madersperger, inventor of the sewing machine (1933, by Philipp), and Siegfried Marcus, one of the inventors of the car (1932, by Seifert).

DER·ZEIT·IHRE·KVNST·
DER·KVNST·IHRE·FREIHEIT·

THE KUNSTHALLE AND SECESSION

At the western end of the park is the new **Kunsthalle Project Space** (open daily 1–7pm; www.KUNSTHALLEwien.at). This striking glass pavilion holds temporary exhibitions of contemporary art.

Star Attraction
● The Secession

Across the road in front of you is the ★★★ **Secession** ㉓ (open Tues–Sun 10am–6pm, Thurs 10am–8pm; www.secession.at), an exhibition space and Vienna's most unusual Art Nouveau building. It was built in 1897–8 as a 'Temple of Art', to plans by Joseph Maria Olbrich, and was completely renovated in 1985. Gustav Klimt designed the metal doors and, in 1902, the stunning *Beethoven Frieze* on display on the lower floor. The cubic foyer of the Secession is crowned by a pierced ball consisting of 3,000 gilt bay leaves, known affectionately as the *Krauthappel* (head of cabbage). Artur Strasser sculpted the *Mark Anthony* group in the garden in 1899–1900.

Papageno on the Theater an der Wien

Over the entrance is the motto 'To Each Time its Art, to Art its Freedom', a ripost from the Secession artists to the hidebound and conservative Academy, based at the nearby Künstlerhaus.

THEATER AN DER WIEN

The **Theater an der Wien** ㉔ is an early Empire-style building which was constructed from 1797 to 1801 for the impresario Emanuel Schikaneder, the librettist of Mozart's *Magic Flute*. It has the most colourful history of all the city's theatres. It was the setting for the premiere of Beethoven's *Fidelio* in 1805, Kleist's *Käthchen von Heilbronn* in 1810 and Grillparzer's *Ahnfrau* in 1817. Most operettas by Johann Strauss and Franz Lehár also saw their first performances here. Only the Papageno Gate in the Millöckergasse remains to give an impression of the original appearance of the theatre. Particularly effective is the pillared portico with the statue group depicting Emanuel Schikaneder as Papageno with his children.

In front of the theatre lies the **Naschmarkt**, the food market, full of stalls and small eateries. Just beyond the market are two Otto Wagner houses (38, the ★ **Majolikahaus**, and 40 Linkewienzeile).

Map on page 66

Further south

To the south of the Academy are three more interesting sights. At Kettenbrückengasse 6 is the **Schuberthaus** 76, where he died (open daily 1pm–4.30pm).

The **Evangelischer Friedhof** on Matzleinsdorfer Platz, with the Grave of the playwright Friedrich Hebbel (1813–63), lies at the end of Wiedner Hauptstrasse. Carrying on, along Triester Strasse, you come to **Spinnerin am Kreuz** (Spinner by the Cross, 1451–2). The carved column, designed by Hans Puchsbaum, is considered to be the most important outdoor Gothic sculpture in Vienna.

Van Dyck's Self Portrait at 15

AKADEMIE DER BILDENDEN KÜNSTE

The **Akademie der Bildenden Künste** 75 (Academy of Fine Arts) was built from 1872 to 1876 to an Italian Renaissance design by Theophil Hansen. Inside, the ceiling paintings of the Great Hall are of particular note. They depict the *Fall of the Titans*, *Venus*, *Prometheus*, *Gaia* and *Uranus* and were completed between 1875 and 1880 by Anselm Feuerbach.

The ★★ **Gemäldegalerie** (the Academy's picture gallery; open Tues–Sun 10am–4pm: www.akademiegalerie.at) has an important collection of paintings. The first room contains the gallery's star exhibit, Heironymous Bosch's *Triptych of the Last Judgement* (1504–8). Also in this room are two wonderful paintings by Lucas Cranach the elder (*The Stigmata of St Francis*, 1501–4, and *Lucretia*, 1532), and Hans Holbein's *Death of Maria* (1518). The second room has Titian's *Tarquin and Lucretia* (n.d.), while the third room, in addition to some superb Ruisdael's, has Van Dyck's exquisite *Self Portrait at 15* (1614–15) and an excellent collection of paintings by Rubens. Another notable exhibit is Rembrant's sensitive *Portrait of a Young Woman* (1632).

The prints and drawings collection contains around 60,000 engravings and drawings as well as watercolours by Thomas Enders from his Brazilian journey of 1817–18; Gothic architectural plans by the master builders of Stephansdom; watercolours of flowers by Daffinger and nature studies by Friedrich Gauermann (by arrangement only, tel: 5881 6225).

SCHILLERPLATZ

In front of the building lies the Schillerplatz, with a park containing the statue of the writer by Johann Schilling (1876). Opposite, on the far side of the Ringstrasse, stands the imposing Goethe Memorial (1900), by Edmund Hellmer.

Mozartplatz (take Karlsgasse and Favoritenstrasse; about 10 minutes' walk) has the delightful Mozart Fountain by Karl Wolk (1905), depicting Tamino and Pamina from *The Magic Flute*.

8: Around Maria-Theresa-Platz

Vienna's huge, 19th-century museum complex around Maria-Theresa-Platz has recently acquired an impressive extension with the opening of the MuseumsQuartier in the old Messepalast, part of the imperial stables designed by Johann Bernhard Fischer von Erlach (1723).

It was decided in 1848 that the state art collections scattered across the city should be gathered together into one single museum complex. However, the project was only realised by 1889. The two massive museum buildings flanking Maria-Theresa-Platz were constructed between 1872 and 1881 by Gottfried Semper, who designed the exterior, and Karl von Hasenauer, who was responsible for the interior

An extensive park was laid out between the two buildings, dominated by a large **monument to Maria Theresa** (1888, by Kaspar Zumbusch). The empress sits on a high pedestal surrounded by a circle of some of the most important men of her time: clockwise, there are equestrian statues of her generals – Daun, Khevenhüller, Traun and Laudon – as well as pedestrian statues of Kaunitz, her Chancellor of State, Van Swieten, her personal physician (the instigator of university reform), Liechtenstein, the creator of the modern artillery and Haugwitz, the administrative reformer.

Star Attraction
● Gemäldegalerie

*Below: Zumbusch's monument to Maria Theresa
Bottom: the Kunsthistorisches Museum staircase*

Map below

The geological galleries in the Naturhistorisches Museum

NATURHISTORISCHES MUSEUM

Looking across the Ringstrasse towards the Hofburg, on your left stands the ★★ **Naturhistorisches Museum 77** (Natural History Museum; open Thur–Mon 9am–6.30pm, Wed 9am–9pm; www.nhm-wien.ac.at). Ceiling paintings by Hans Canon in the foyer show the cycle of life. The museum's huge collections range from prehistoric and anthropological displays and minerals to animal and plant exhibits. Much of the labelling is in German only, though this is being changed as the displays are redesigned. For children there is a crèche offering a wide variety of supervised play facilities. The café on the first floor is very pleasant.

MUSEUM EXHIBITS

The ground floor displays show the musem's geological and prehistoric collections. Of particular interest are the geological exhibits, which include precious stones from Maria Theresa's private collection, the meteorite collection (one of the largest and most important in the world), and fossils.

The prehistoric collections are also impressive. Perhaps the most important artefact held in the museum is the ***Venus of Willendorf***, a fertility symbol dating from c 20,000 BC. Other fascinating exhibits include objects from the Celtic burial ground near Hallstatt (early Iron Age, 800–400 BC) and Langobard finds. At the end of the prehistoric galleries is an excellent series of interactive displays representing the evolution of humans.

The first floor is given over to zoology. The most attractive displays here are the terrariums with live fish, amphibians and reptiles, arranged around the central atrium. Apart from a very good hands-on display of microscopes and microbiology, much of the zoological displays are the usual depressing array of dead and stuffed mammals and birds, which only serve to remind us how much more beautiful the living versions are.

ROUTE 8

0   300 m
0   300 yards

KUNSTHISTORISCHES MUSEUM

On the far side of the Maria Theresa Memorial lies one of the jewels in the crown of Vienna, the ★★★ **Kunsthistorisches Museum** ❼❽ (Museum of Fine Arts; open Tues–Sun 10am–6pm, Thur 10am–9pm; www.khm.at). A number of famous artists worked together on the ornamentation of the interior: Viktor Tilgner, Hans Makart, Michael Munkácsy, Ernst and Gustav Klimt, and Franz Matsch, to name but a few. The huge collection of paintings, applied arts and archaeological artefacts can be overwhelming, and the museum is best seen over a couple of visits, rather than in one go.

GROUND FLOOR

The **Egyptian and Near Eastern Collections** are to the right of the main entrance. The newly renovated galleries are beautifully decorated with ancient Egyptian motifs and are well laid out. The

Star Attractions
- **Naturhistorisches Museum**
- **Kunsthistorisches Museum**

Museum staircase
On the main landing stands a marble group by Antonio Canova dating from before 1819; it shows *Theseus vanquishing the Centaur*. Adorning the stairwell ceiling is *The Apotheosis of the Fine Arts* by Michael Munkácsy, which is surrounded by medallions by Hans Makart portraying famous artists with their favourite models.

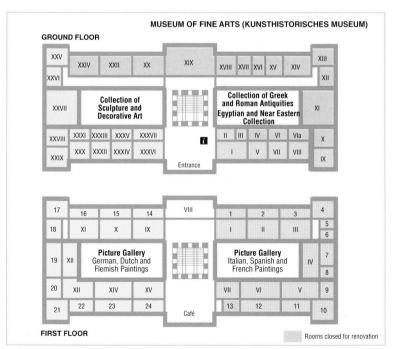

MUSEUM OF FINE ARTS (KUNSTHISTORISCHES MUSEUM)

GROUND FLOOR

XXV | XXIV | XXII | XX | XIX | XVIII | XVII | XVI | XV | XIV | XIII
XXVI | | | | | | | | | | XII
XXVII | Collection of Sculpture and Decorative Art | | | | Collection of Greek and Roman Antiquities / Egyptian and Near Eastern Collection | | | | | XI
XXVIII | XXXI | XXXIII | XXXV | XXXVII | II | III | IV | VIa | | X
XXIX | XXX | XXXII | XXXIV | XXXVI | I | V | VII | VIII | | IX

ℹ Entrance

FIRST FLOOR

17 | 16 | 15 | 14 | VIII | 1 | 2 | 3 | 4
18 | XI | X | IX | | I | II | III | 5 / 6
19 | XII | Picture Gallery / German, Dutch and Flemish Paintings | | | Picture Gallery / Italian, Spanish and French Paintings | | IV | 7 / 8
20 | XII | XIV | XV | | VII | VI | V | 9
21 | 22 | 23 | 24 | Café | 13 | 12 | 11 | 10

Rooms closed for renovation

Map on page 72

collection has a good selection of Egyptian arte-facts, from prehistoric times until well into the Christian era. As well as an excellent collection of sculpture (Room IX has some wonderful 4th Dynasty/c. 2,500 BC, heads, and a statue of Sethos I, 19th Dynasty/c. 1300 BC; the carving of the folded clothing is remarkable), off to the side of the first room is a reconstruction of a 4th Dynasty cult chamber from the pyramid of Cheops at Giza. Look out also for the famous 11th/12th Dynasty (c. 2000 BC) faïence model of a hippopotamus.

GREEK AND ROMAN ANTIQUITIES

The extensive collection of **Greek and Roman Antiquities** is closed at present as the galleries undergo renovation. The new galleries promise to be just as impressive as the new Egyptian ones, and a fitting setting for star exhibits such as the *Cameo of a Ptolemaic Royal Couple* (278–269 BC) and the stunning Germanic jewellery dating from the Time of the Great Migration (c. 400 AD).

The **Sculpture and Decorative Arts Gallery** *(Plastik und Kunstgewerbe)*, also currently closed for renovation, lies opposite the Egyptian galleries. The most important item on display here is the famous salt cellar by Benvenuto Cellini (mid-16th century). Other interesting pieces include a 14th century ivory altarpiece and some beautiful Dutch early-16th century tapestries. There are also numerous Italian bronzes and quartz crystal vessels (14th–18th centuries).

Velázquez
The Museum's collection of paintings by the Spanish painter Velázquez (1599–1660) is quite stunning, and constitutes one of the best collections of the artist's work outside Spain. Displayed in Room 10 they include: three portraits of the *Infanta Margarita Isolde* (in pink, white and blue, 1653–4, 1656 and 1659 respectively); *Philip IV of Spain* (1632); the *Infanta Maria Theresa* (1652–3); and the sensitive *Infante Felipe Próspero* (1659).

Raphael's Madonna of the Meadows

THE PICTURE GALLERY

The rooms and cabinets of the famous ★★★ **Picture Gallery** occupy the first floor. They contain works by Italian, Spanish and French masters in the West Wing, whilst those by Dutch, Flemish, German and English artists occupy the East Wing. The museum's excellent café, in what must be one of the best locations in Vienna, occupies the space under the building's central dome. The summary below contains only a selection of the works on view *(see plan, page 73)*.

ITALIAN PAINTING

Room I contains the gallery's collection of works by **Titian** (1487–1576), including *Ecce Homo* (1543) and *Woman in Furs* (1535). The paintings in Room 1, of the Northern Italian Early Renaissance, slightly predate those of Titian and include works by **Mantegna** (*St Sebastian*, 1457–9) and **Bellini** (*Young Woman at her Toilet*, 1515).

The High and Late Renaissance of Venice is represented in Rooms II and 2. Here there are paintings by **Giorgione** (*Laura*, 1506, and *The Three Philosophers*, 1508–9), **Palma Vecchio** (*Maria with Child and Saints*, 1520–22), and **Veronese** (the *Anointing of David*, 1555, and *Judith with the Head of Holofernes*, 1582).

Room 3 has works from the High Renaissance of Central Italy, represented by **Parmigiano** (*Painting of a Young Woman*, 1530) and **Correggio** (*Madonna and Child*, 1512–14), while Room III is devoted to Venetian Mannerism, chiefly works by **Tintoretto** (including *Susanna in the Bath*, 1555–6, and *Sebastiano Venier*, 1571).

One of the gallery's most important works is found in Room 4, Raphael's exquisite *Madonna of the Meadows* (1505–6). Also here is Fra Bartholomeo's *Christ in the Temple* (1516).

Room IV contains *The Martyrdom of St Peter* (1570) by the Florentine painter and writer **Vasari**, and Room V is has superb examples of

Star Attraction
● The Picture Gallery

Below: The Infanta Margarita Isolde *by Velázquez*
Bottom: Bruegel's Hunters in the Snow

Map
on page
72

Bruegel
Room X holds the world's largest collection of works by the Flemish artist Peter Bruegel the Elder (1526–69), who painted landscapes and finely observed depictions of village life. This phenomenal display includes: the *Village Wedding* (1568) and *Village Dance* (1568–9); the *Battle Between Carnival and Lent* (1559); *Childrens' Games* (1559); the *Tower of Babel* (1563); and *Hunters in the Snow* (1565).

the work of **Caravaggio** (1571–1610). These include *Christ with the Crown of Thorns* (1603–4), the *Madonna of the Rosary* and *David with the Head of Goliath* (both 1606–7).

Other works to look out for include: the Florentine Mannerist painter Bronzino's *Holy Family with St Anna and St John* (1540, Room 7); and the French artist Poussin's *Storming of the Temple in Jerusalem* (1638–9, Room 11).

NORTHERN EUROPEAN PAINTING

The treasures in Room 14 include the *Johannes Altar* by **Memling** (1485–90), a double-sided section of an altarpiece (1480–90) by **Bosch**, and **van Eyck**'s portraits of *Cardinal Niccolò Albergati* (1435) and *The Goldsmith Jan de Leeuw* (1436).

Pass through Room 15, with its *Lucretia* (1520–5) by **van Cleve**, into Room 16 with its superb collection of paintings by **Dürer**. Here you can find *Maria with a Child at Her Breast* (1503), the *Martyrdom of the 10,000 Christians* (1508), and the *Landauer Altar* (1511).

Rooms 17 and 18 have a wonderful array of works by **Cranach** and **Holbein**. Of the former, look out for *Paradise* (1530), *Judith with the Head of Holofernes* (1530), and *Three Princesses* (1535). Works by Holbein include his portraits of *Jane Seymour* (1536–7) and *Dr John Chambers* (1543).

Other particularly strong collections include Room XII's pictures by **van Dyke** (*Portrait of a Man*, 1620–21, and *Painting of an Old Woman*, 1634), and the astounding three rooms of works by **Rubens** (XI, XIII and 20). Look for the *Woman with a Fan* (1612–14), *The Four Continents* (1615) and *The Little Fur* (1636–8).

Room XV, notable for its paintings by **Rembrant** (1606–69), includes the touching twin portraits of a man and a woman (1632), the *Painter's Mother as the Prophetess Hanna* (1639), and four self portraits (1652–7). Off to the side, in Room 24, is *The Artist's Studio* by **Vermeer** (1665–6).

MUSEUMS QUARTIER

Volkstheater
Burggasse
VOLKS-THEATER
Naturhistorisches Museum (Museum of Natural History)
Kindergarten, Institut für Umweltwissenschaften
HOF 6
Architekturzentrum Wien
Breite Gasse
HOF 5
MUMOK
Museumstraße
MQ Ticket-Center
Entrance
KUNSTHALLE wien
HOF 1
HOF 4
Halle E+G
Schweighofergasse
MQ Visitor Center
Leopold Museum
wienXtra-Kindermuseum
Tanzquartier Wien
HOF 2
ZOOM Kindermuseum
HOF 3
Mariahilfer Str.
ART CULT CENTER TABAK MUSEUM
0   150 m
0   150 yards

THE MUSEUMSQUARTIER

The new ★★★ **MuseumsQuartier** (visitor and ticket centre open Sat–Wed 10am–7pm, Thur–Fri 10am–9pm; www.mqw.at), a huge cultural complex, includes, as well as those galleries described below, the **Architecturzentrum Wien** (Vienna Architecture Centre; open daily 10am–7pm; www.azw.at) and **Kunsthalle Wien** (open daily 10am–7pm, Thur 10am–10pm; www.KUNSTHALLEwien.at), both of which hold temporary exhibitions. **Tanzquartier Wien** is a performance space and study centre for contemporary dance (www.tqw.at), while the **Tabakmuseum** (Tobacco Museum) is for enthusiasts only.

Star Attractions
● **MuseumsQuartier**
● **MUMOK**

Below: the Leopold Museum
Bottom: MUMOK

MUMOK

The large building that dominates the northwestern end of the piazza is ★★ **MUMOK** (Museum of Modern Art; open Tues–Sun 10am–6pm, Thur 10am–9pm; www.mumok.at). This houses an extensive collection of largely post-war and contemporary art. Level 1 has a number of pre-war works, including Kandinsky's *Obstinate* (1933) and De Chirico's *Au Bord de la Mer* (1925). However, the most interesting exhibits are those by the **Viennese Actionists**, a 1960s group that included Güter Bros, Otto Muehl, Hermann Nitsch and Rudolf Schwarzkogler. They performed their happenings to shock conservative post-war Austrian society.

Map on page 76

Below: Schiele's Moa the Dancer
Bottom: the Attersee by Klimt

Moving up, Level 3 has displays of 1960s Minimalism, works by Arte Povera, Concept Art, as well as examples of the Identity Art of the 1990s. Level 4, the level at which you enter, is perhaps more impressive, with its huge canvases by Gilbert and George. Level 5 has the museum's café.

Works from the 1980s and '90s are found on Level 6, as well as a highly minimalist 2001 installation by Ilya Kabakov. Also here is a collection of derivative pieces by Central European artists (1960s–present day), including an elegant mobile by Karel Malich (1973–4).

Level 7 concentrates on Fluxus and Nouveau Realisme, with many pieces by Daniel Spoerri and the inevitable Yves Klein *Monochrome Blue* (1961).The largely American Pop Art and Photorealist works are found on Level 8. These include Lichtenstein's *Red Horseman* (1974), and a couple of pieces by Jasper Johns (*Two Flags*, 1959, and *Target*, 1967–9).

THE LEOPOLD MUSEUM

The ★★★ **Leopold Museum** (open Wed–Mon 10am–7pm, Fri 10am–9pm; www.leopoldmuseum.org) stands opposite MUMOK, its gleaming white limestone cladding contrasting with the latter's grey basalt. The exhibits, taken from the collection of the Viennese couple Rudolf and Elizabeth

Leopold, comprise some of the most important works of 19th and 20th-century Austrian art. The new building is beautifully designed, allowing natural light into many of the galleries via a central light well. There's a café on the first floor.

The lowest floor, Basement 2, houses the graphics collection and examples of non-Western art, including some wonderful Dan masks from Guinea. Of the graphics, particularly notable works include Schiele's *Moa the Dancer* (1911) and *Edith Schiele Dying* (1918), and Kokoschka's poster for the Summer Theatre in Art Exhibition (1908). Moving up, the next floor has some fine 19th-century Japanese prints, and posters for the 8th, 14th and 15th Secession exhibitions. Also here are the 19th-century Austrian oils and graphics. The later oils all show the influence of French painting of the time, as in Cecil van Haauen's *Courtesan in Pink* (n.d.), though the two works by Tina Blau, *Apple Blossom* (1894) and *Scene in the Prater* (1910–15), are more adventurous.

THE 20TH-CENTURY COLLECTIONS

The museum's displays of Jugendstil and Secessionist works are on the ground floor. Here there are some impressive canvases by Klimt, especially *Death and Life* (1911–15) and the earlier *Attersee* (1901). Two other fine paintings are, Gerstl's *Portrait of Henrika Cohn* (1908), and Andri's *Woman in a Red Dress* (1917). Also look out for Moser's sketch for the angel window in Otto Wagner's Am Steinhof church.

On the second floor the most striking works are the large paintings by Albin Egger-Lienz (1868–1926), including *The Dark Wood* (1895) and *The Reapers* (1918). There are also a couple of rooms devoted to Austrian painting since 1945.

The stunning collection of Expressionist and inter-war painting is on the top floor. The real gems here are works by Schiele (including *Seated Male Nude: Self Portrait*, 1910, *Reclining Woman*, 1917, and *Three Standing Women*, 1918), Kokoschka (*Self Portrait, One Hand on Face*, 1918–19), and Max Oppenheimer (*Tilla Durieux*, 1912).

Star Attraction
● Leopold Museum

> **Republican monument**
> In the park that stands on the corner between the Burgring and Dr Karl-Lueger-Ring is the Monument to the Republic. The three busts forming the memorial, erected in 1928 to mark the tenth anniversary of the founding of the Austrian Republic, represent (from left to right) Jakob Reumann, Viktor Adler and Ferdinand Hanusch, the founders of the republican form of government in Austria.

Viktor Adler on the Monument to the Republic

Map on page 72

TRAUTSON PALACE

Continuing along Museumstrasse you will pass the Volkstheater. By the theatre stands a monument to the poet Ferdinand Raimund (1898, by Franz Vogl). Nearby stands the former **Trautson Palace** ⑧⓪, now the Ministry of Justice. The mansion was built in 1710–12 as a garden palais following plans by Johann Bernhard Fischer von Erlach. Nowadays it is considered to be the finest of his secular buildings in Vienna.

The Justizpalast

AUERSPERG PALACE

The **Auersperg Palace** ⑧①, constructed in 1706, is thought to have been the work of Johann Lukas von Hildebrandt. During the 19th century it was redesigned in the Classical style. On the Schmerlingplatz nearby is the recently-restored **Justizpalast** ⑧② (Palace of Justice). Constructed between 1875 and 1881 after plans by Alexander Wielemans, it was damaged by fire during the political unrest of 1927 and rebuilt in its present form. The large marble hall contains a huge statue of *Justice* by Pendl; above the arches of the arcades can be seen the coats of arms of the Austro-Hungarian crown territories. (To gain entry pass through the security cubicles just inside the entrance.)

ALONG MARIAHILFERSTRASSE

There are three interesting sights along Mariahilferstrasse. The church of **Mariahilferkloster** ⑧③ was founded in 1660 and rebuilt in 1686–1723. The ceiling paintings date from 1759–60, painted under the supervision of Paul Troger.

Further on is the **Hofmobiliendepot** ⑧④ (open daily 9am–5pm). This contains furniture, carpets, pictures and other items from the Baroque to the end of the Biedermeier periods. The Imperial Throne (19th-century) is also on view here.

The last of the three is the **Haydn Museum** ⑧⑤ (open Tues–Sat 9am–12.15pm, 1–4.30pm). Josef Haydn lived here from 1793 to 1809, and original manuscripts, letters and personal memorabilia afford a glimpse of the composer's life and works.

9: Parlament to the Freud Museum

Map
on page
82

Begin at the **Parlament** ❸ on the Ringstrasse. Designed in the Hellenistic style, the Parlament building is one of the architect Theophil Hansen's most impressive works. Constructed between 1873 and 1883, it was originally the meeting place of the Imperial Council; today, it houses the sessions of the National and Federal Councils.

Flags flying from the roof indicate that the assembly is in session. (Guided tours: Jun–Sept: Mon–Fri hourly 9am–3pm; Oct–Jun: Mon–Thur 11am and 3pm, Fri hourly 11am–3pm; no tours when parliament is in session; tel: 40110-2715; www.parlament.gv.at)

In front of the main facade stands the Pallas-Athene-Brunnen (1898–1902), by Karl Kundmann. At Athene's feet are seated the allegorical figures sculpted by Josef Tautenhayn, of Legislation (right) and Administration (left); below them lie two groups of river deities (in front, the Danube and the Inn; to the rear, the Elbe and the Vltava).

Parliamentary pomp
The approach ramp is adorned with two equestrian groups and seated figures of statesmen and historians of antiquity. The tympanum above the portico, which is supported by 10-m (33-ft) columns, is decorated with a relief by Edmund Hellmer portraying *The Emperor as Law-Giver summoning the 17 Crown Provinces*. Behind the columns is a frieze on a gold background depicting *The Homage of the Peoples of the Austrian Empire* by Lebiedzki.

THE VOLKSGARTEN

The **Volksgarten** ❸ was laid out in 1823 on the site of the demolished Castle Bastion. It is famous for its delightful rose garden. Amongst the most

Tautenhayn's statues in front of the Parlament

Map below

notable sights are the Temple of Theseus, by Peter Nobile (1820–3), in front of which stands an elegant bronze statue of a *Young Athlete* (1921), by Josef Müllner. Not far away stands the attractive fountain group *Faun and Nymph* (1880), by Viktor Tilgner.

On the park railings you can see a memorial to Julius Raab (1891–1964), completed in 1962 by Gustinus Ambrosi. As Federal Chancellor he played a crucial role in the drafting and signing of the Austrian State Treaty of 1955.

Memorial to a princess
Also in the Volksgarten is a memorial to the Empress Elizabeth, who was murdered in 1898 (1907, by Hans Bitterlich), and another to Franz Grillparzer (1889, by Karl Kundmann); the flanking walls are decorated with reliefs depicting various scenes from six of the playwright's dramas: (from left to right) *Die Ahnfrau*, *A Dream is Life*, *King Ottakar – His Rise and Fall*, *Sappho*, *Medea* and *The Waves of Sea and Love*.

THE BURGTHEATER

The ★ **Burgtheater** ⑧, affectionately known as the 'Burg', is one of the most important stages in the German-speaking world. It was built in the Italian High Renaissance style between 1874 and 1888 to a design by Gottfried Semper and Karl von Hasenauer. It replaced the National and Court Theatre *(see page 38)*, built on the Michaelerplatz in 1776 under the patronage of Joseph II.

The central facade is decorated with a relief portraying *Bacchus in Procession*; the balustrade shows the figure of Apollo between Melpomene (the Muse of Tragedy) and Thalia (the Muse of

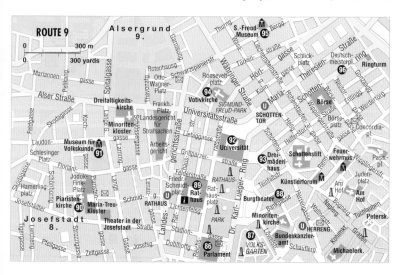

Comedy). Above the main windows are the busts of famous men of letters by Viktor Tilgner. On the low side wings, symbolic figures represent Love, Hate, Heroism, Egoism, Humility and Domineering Behaviour. The magnificent staircases are enriched with frescoes by Ernst and Gustav Klimt; the interior is extravagantly adorned with Baroque-inspired stucco ornamentation. (Guided tours: Jul–Aug daily 2 and 3pm; Sept–Jun daily 3 pm; tel: 51444-4140; www.burgtheater.at)

The Rathaus with the Christmas market in front

THE RATHAUS

The imposing ★ **Rathaus** ❸❾ (New Town Hall) was built between 1872 and 1883 in the neo-Gothic style by Friedrich von Schmidt. It houses the offices of the municipal administration and the city archives and library.

Along the promenade you will see the statues (1867) of eight important personalities in Vienna's history. In the Town Hall Gardens in front of the Town Hall are a number of prominent memorials: to the federal president Dr Karl Renner (1967, by Alfred Hrdlicka), to the 'waltz kings' Johann Strauss the Elder and Josef Lanner (1905, by Franz Seifert), to the mayor and subsequent federal president Theodor Körner (1963) and to the landscape artist Ferdinand Waldmüller (1913, by Engelhart).

PIARISTENKIRCHE

To the west of the Rathaus is the **Piaristenkirche** ❾⓿. Designed in 1698 by Johann Lukas von Hildebrandt, the church was completed in 1753. It has particularly fine frescoes (1752–3) by Franz Anton Maulpertsch. The central dome depicts a *Coronation of the Virgin Mary* with episodes from the Old and New Testaments. Above the organ is a *Fall of the Angels*, and on the vaulted roof above the choir an *Assumption of the Virgin Mary*. Karl Rahl did the altar painting depicting *The Marriage of the Virgin* (1841). In front of the church is a column erected in 1713 to mark the end of an epidemic of plague.

Map on page 82

Just to the north of the Piaristenkirche is the ★**Museum für Volkskunde** ⑨ (Museum of Folklore; open Tues–Sun 9am–5pm; www.volkskunde-museum.at). Located in the Palais Schönborn (built by by Johann Lukas von Hildebrandt in 1708–13), the museum provides a survey of Austrian traditions and customs, as well as holding temporary exhibitions covering broader themes.

THE UNIVERSITY

Returning to the Ringstrasse, next door to the Town Hall Gardens is the main **Universität** ⑨ (university) building; this is the oldest German-speaking university, constructed between 1873 and 1883 in the Italian Renaissance style to house the *Alma Mater Rudolfina*, established in 1365 by Duke Rudolf IV the Founder. It houses, amongst other departments, the faculties of philosophy, theology and law. The main courtyard contains memorials to famous professors.

> **Schubert connection?**
> According to the musical play *The Dreimäderlhaus*, with music largely by Franz Schubert, the composer was a frequent guest here. But one should seldom take at face value what one sees in musical plays: there is no proven link between Schubert and the house. It was apparently chosen as the setting for the play simply because of its obviously romantic atmosphere.

On the far side of the Ringstrasse lie the ruins of the former Mölkerbastei fortress. In front is a memorial crowned with a gilded Athena Niké (1890) to Liebenberg, the mayor who led the defence of Vienna during the second Turkish siege in 1683.

On the site of the ramparts you can visit the **Dreimäderlhaus** ⑨ (House of the Three Girls). Dating from 1803, this is a typical middle-class dwelling built in the style known as 'Josephine Classicism'. It now houses the shop of the Viennese shoe maker, Ludwig Reiter.

The Dreimäderlhaus

Nearby stands the **Pasqualatihaus**. Built in 1797, it was the home for several years of Ludwig van Beethoven and is believed to be the place where he composed the opera *Fidelio* (open Tues–Sun 9am–12.15pm, 1–4.30pm).

THE VOTIVKIRCHE

From the intersection between the Ringstrasse and the Schottengasse, known as Schottentor (Scottish Gate), the vista opens up to reveal the ★**Votivkirche** ⑨. It was built to commemorate a failed attempt on the life of Emperor Francis Joseph in 1853. The most important neo-Gothic building in Vienna, the church (built by Heinrich Ferstel) was constructed in 1856–79 and has twin spires 10m (33ft) high. On the left in the baptismal chapel stands the late-Gothic tomb of Count Niklas von Salm, which is presumed to date from about 1530. The count was the commander of the Viennese troops during the first Turkish siege of 1529. On the opposite side of the nave is a carved altar, the so-called Antwerp Altar, which features remarkable reliefs depicting the Passion of Christ (end of the 15th century).

THE FREUD MUSEUM

Just across the road from the Votive Church, at Berggasse 19, is the ★★ **Sigmund Freud Museum ⑨** (open daily 9am–5pm; http://freud.0t.or.at; *see page 12*). Set in Freud's former home and consulting rooms, the museum is dedicated to the life and work of the controversial psychoanalyst. As the headquarters of the Sigmund Freud Society, the museum also has an impressive archive (open to readers by appointment only, tel: 319 1596).

A remnant of the Austro-Hungarian Empire can be found further east, on Deutschmeister-Platz. The **Deutschmeister Monument ⑨** was erected in 1906 to honour the imperial regiment.

Star Attraction
● **Sigmund Freud Museum**

Below: the nave of the Votivkirche
Bottom: Freud's apartments

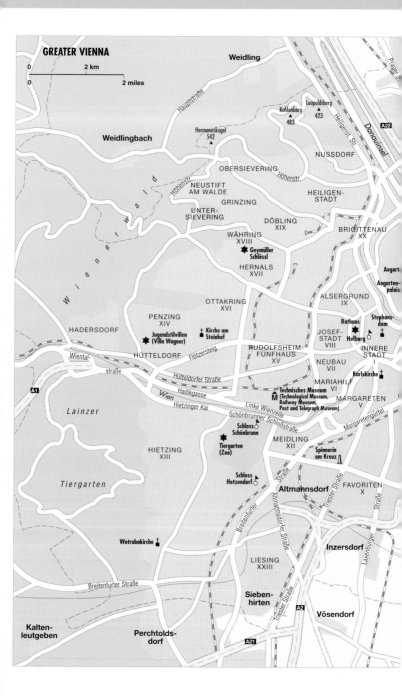

GREATER VIENNA

Weidling

0   2 km
0   2 miles

Hauptstraße

Weidlingbach

Hermannskogel
542 ▲

Kahlenberg
483 ▲

Leopoldsberg
423 ▲

Heiligenst. Str.

Donauinsel

A22

Prager Str.

NUSSDORF

OBERSIEVERING

Höhenstr.

Höhenstr.

NEUSTIFT
AM WALDE

GRINZING

HEILIGEN-
STADT

UNTER-
SIEVERING

DÖBLING
XIX

WÄHRING
XVIII

Geymüller
Schlössl

BRIGITTENAU
XX

HERNALS
XVII

Augart...

Augarten-
palais

W i e n e r w a l d

OTTAKRING
XVI

ALSERGRUND
IX

HADERSDORF

PENZING
XIV

Jugendstilvillen
(Villa Wagner)

† Kirche am
Steinhof

Rathaus
✦

Stephans-
dom

JOSEF-
STADT
VIII

Hofburg

INNERE
STADT
I

RUDOLFSHEIM-
FÜNFHAUS
XV

HÜTTELDORF

Flötzersteig

Wiental-

straße

Hütteldorfer Straße

NEUBAU
VII

Karlskirche †

Wien

Hadikgasse

MARIAHILF
VI

Technisches Museum
(Technological Museum,
Railway Museum,
Post and Telegraph Museum)

M

Hietzinger Kai

Linke Wienzeile

MARGARETEN
V

Lainzer

Schönbrunner Schloßstraße

Margaretengürtel

Schloss
Schönbrunn

MEIDLING
XII

Spinnerin
am Kreuz

HIETZING
XIII

Tiergarten
(Zoo)
✦

Tiergarten

Schloss
Hetzendorf

Altmannsdorf

FAVORITEN
X

Breitenfurter Straße

Altmannsdorfer Straße

Trieser Straße

Straße

Laxenburger Straße

Wotrubakirche †

Inzersdorf

LIESING
XXIII

Sieben-
hirten

A2

Vösendorf

Kalten-
leutgeben

Perchtolds-
dorf

A21

A1

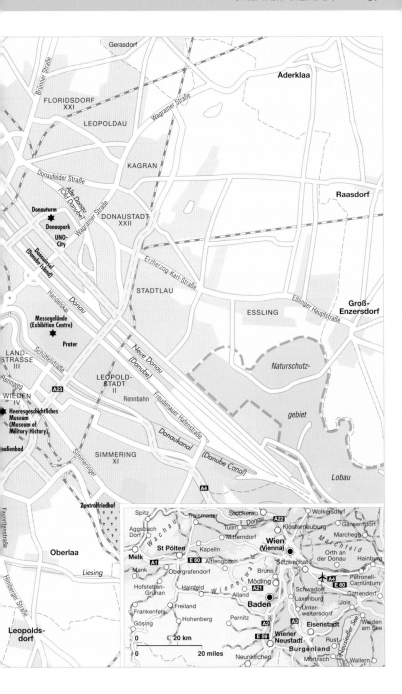

Gerasdorf

Aderklaa

FLORIDSDORF
XXI

Brünner Straße

LEOPOLDAU

Wagramer Straße

KAGRAN

Donaufelder Straße

Raasdorf

Alte Donau
(Old Danube)

Donauturm ★

Donaupark

UNO-
City

DONAUSTADT
XXII

Wagramer Straße

Donauinsel
(Danube Island)

Handelskai

Donau

Erzherzog-Karl-Straße

STADTLAU

Groß-
Enzersdorf

ESSLING

Eßlinger Hauptstraße

Messegelände
(Exhibition Centre) ★

Prater

Schüttelstraße

Neue Donau
(Danube)

LAND-
STRASSE
III

Rennweg

A23

WIEDEN
IV

LEOPOLD-
STADT
II

Rennbahn

Freudenauer Hafenstraße

Naturschutz-

★ Heeresgeschichtliches
Museum
(Museum of
Military History)

nalienbad

Simmeringer

SIMMERING
XI

Donaukanal

Donaukanal
(Danube Canal)

gebiet

A4

Lobau

Favoritenstraße

Zentralfriedhof

† † †
† †
† † †

Spitz

Traismauer

Stockerau

Wolkersdorf

Wachau

Tulln

Donau

A22

Klosterneuburg

Gänserndorf

Oberlaa

Aggsbach
Dorf

Mitterndorf

**Wien
(Vienna)**

Marchfeld

Marchegg

Liesing

St Pölten

Kapelln

Altlengbach

Orth an
der Donau

Hainburg

Melk

A1

E 60

Obergrafendorf

Brunn

Schwechat

Himberger Straße

Mank

Mödling

Schwadorf

A4

E 60

Petronell-
Carnuntum

Hofstetten-
Grünau

Hainfeld

Wienerwald

Alland

Laxenburg

Gattendorf

**Leopolds-
dorf**

Frankenfels

Freiland

Baden

Unter-
waltersdorf

Jois

Neusiedler See

Gösing

Hohenberg

Pernitz

A2

A3

Eisenstadt

Weiden
am See

0   20 km

**Wiener
Neustadt**

Rust

0   20 miles

E 59

Burgenland

Neunkirchen

Mörbisch

Wallern

Map
on pages
86–7

Greater Vienna

The outer districts (Nos X–XXIII) of Vienna have many sights well worth a visit. All the places described below are easily reached on the city's fast and efficient public transport.

SCHLOSS SCHÖNBRUNN

The ★★★ **Schloss Schönbrunn** (www.schoenbrunn.at), which lies about 6km (4 miles) from the city centre, is best reached by underground (U4 to Schönbrunn or Hietzing). The park is open 6am–dusk (6.30am in winter); the palace is open Apr–Jun and Sept–Oct 8.30am–5pm, Jul–Aug 8.30am–7pm, Nov–Mar 8.30am–4.30pm. Of the two palace tours, the Grand Tour (of 40 rooms) is better value as it gives you access to the audience chambers of Maria Theresa. A useful audioguide is included in the price of entry.

The Schönbrunn garden facade and staircase

PALACE HISTORY

The *Kattermühle* (mill) that originally stood on the site was mentioned in records for the first time in 1311. A castle, the Katterburg, was added in 1471. In 1568 the property passed to Maximilian II; he had it converted into a hunting lodge and later added a zoo. In 1619 Emperor Matthew, whilst hunting, discovered a 'beautiful spring' *(Schöner Brunnen)*. This supplied the palace's water until the end of the 18th century.

The hunting lodge was destroyed by the Turks in 1683 and a grandiose new palace, intended to outshine Versailles, was designed by Johann Bernhard Fischer von Erlach. It was to have been built on the Gloriette Hill, but costly military campaigns thwarted the project. A less elaborate building, in which Emperor Joseph I (1705–11) frequently stayed, was completed by 1700.

Joseph's successor Charles VI neglected the building, and during his reign only a number of uncoordinated projects were undertaken under Josef Emanuel Fischer von Erlach. It was the Empress Maria Theresa (1740–80) who had

Schönbrunn completed. In 1744 she commissioned Nicolaus Paccassi to rebuild and extend the palace, which was completed in 1750. By 1765 the interior was also finished in accordance with Paccassi's design. The park was laid out initially in the French style by Jean Trehet in 1705–6. Its present appearance dates from 1753–75 and was the work of Ferdinand von Hohenberg. Most of the ★ **garden statues** are by Wilhelm Bayer. The Neptune Fountain was added in 1780.

From the reign of Maria Theresa, Schönbrunn became a favourite residence of the Imperial family. Its 1441 rooms and halls were needed to maintain the court. Some 390 of these were residential apartments and audience chambers and there were 139 kitchens. Almost 1,000 people lived in the vast complex, which together with its park covers 176 hectares (435 acres). Emperor Francis Joseph I was born here, and died here in 1916. It was here, too, that Emperor Charles I renounced the right to rule in 1918, thus marking the end of the monarchy.

Star Attraction
● **Schloss Schönbrunn**

Napoleonic memories
When Napoleon I occupied Vienna in 1805–6 he used Schönbrunn as his headquarters. During the Vienna Congress at the end of the Napoleonic Wars, in 1814–15, the palace was the setting for glittering celebrations. Napoleon's only son, who later became Duke of Reichstadt, also lived and died here.

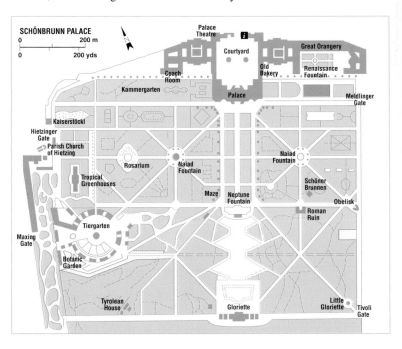

SCHÖNBRUNN PALACE

0 ___ 200 m
0 ___ 200 yds

N

Palace Theatre
Courtyard
Great Orangery
Coach Room
Old Bakery
Renaissance Fountain
Kammergarten
Palace
Meldlinger Gate
Kaiserstöckl
Hietzinger Gate
Parish Church of Hietzing
Rosarium
Naiad Fountain
Naiad Fountain
Tropical Greenhouses
Maze
Neptune Fountain
Schöner Brunnen
Obelisk
Roman Ruin
Maxing Gate
Tiergarten
Botanic Garden
Tyrolean House
Gloriette
Little Gloriette
Tivoli Gate

Map
on page
89

THE PALACE

The ★★ **palace** itself is 175m (574ft) long and 55m (180ft) wide. On the courtyard and garden side it boasts two similar, richly decorated Baroque facades. Two staircases bordered by Rococo balustrades lead up to the balcony terraces, situated above a carriage thoroughfare with five magnificent wrought-iron gateways. The hall, decorated with two statue groups portraying Hercules (c. 1700, by Adrian de Vries), leads on the right to the sleeping quarters, with a large number of fine works of art.

Below: a garden statue
Bottom: the palace

FIRST FLOOR

Ascending the Blue Staircase, with a ceiling painting depicting *The Apotheosis of Joseph I* (early 18th-century), you will reach the rooms open to the public. Of particular interest are: the Death Chamber of Emperor Francis Joseph, the Hall of Mirrors (in which the six-year-old Mozart performed for the Empress Maria Theresa), the Chinese Round Cabinet (the conference room of the Empress and her Chancellor of State Kaunitz), the Great Gallery and the Small Gallery, adorned with ceiling paintings by Gregorio Guglielmi (1759–61; frescoes depicting *The Seven Years War* or *The Clement Rule of Maria Theresa*), the Ceremonial Hall (with the portrait of the empress by Martin van Meytens), the notable Gobelin

Room with its tapestries, and the confusingly ornate Room of Millions (Maria Theresa's private salon), as well as the Napoleon Room, which recalls the Napoleonic occupation of the city.

The **Bergl-Zimmer** (open only with a 'VIP Pass', Apr–Oct) are elaborately decorated rooms with *trompe l'oeil* landscape paintings by Johann Bergl, a pupil of Paul Troger (1780). The Palace Chapel is close by (entry by appointment only), with a high altar adorned with *The Marriage of the Virgin Mary*, a painting by Paul Troger and *The Suffering Madonna*, a relief by Raphael Donner. The frescoes are by Daniel Gran; the high altar is the work of Franz Kohl.

In front of the palace is the 24,000sq-m (260,000sq-ft) **Courtyard**. The main gateway is flanked by two obelisks. These were given French imperial eagles in 1809, after Napoleon's victory. On the right is the Rococo Schönbrunn Court Theatre, fitted out by Ferdinand von Hohenberg in 1766–7. The courtyard has two large fountains: on the right are depicted the allegorical figures of the the Crown Lands of Transylvania, Galicia and Lodomeria (by Franz Anton Zauner); on the left are J Hagenauer's allegoric portrayals of the Danube, Inn and Ems.

In the ★ **Wagenburg** (Coach Room; open Apr–Oct: daily 9am–6pm, Nov–Mar: Tues–Sun 10am–4pm) is a large collection of imperial coaches, state carriages, sedan chairs and sledges from 1690 to 1917. Near the palace's left wing is a **Renaissance Fountain**, dating from the 16th century.

FOUNTAINS AND RUINS

At the far side of the flower beds, flanked by rows of statues, is the ★ **Neptune Fountain** by Franz Anton Zauner (1780). It represents Thetis asking Neptune to grant her son Achilles a safe voyage to Troy. On the left is the ★ '**Roman Ruin**', completed by Ferdinand von Hohenberg in 1778.

The Egyptian-inspired **obelisk** dates from 1777. Instead of hieroglyphics, the carvings depict scenes from the history of the Habsburg family. Not far from the obelisk lies the **Schöner Brunnen**. The

Star Attraction
● **The palace**

Floral delights
Visitors interested in botany are recommended to visit the ★ **Tropical Greenhouses**, which contain a riot of tropical plants, and the **Botanic Garden**, which contains memorials to Emperor Joseph I and Francis I of Lorraine. The Kaiserstöckl (1777) was the summer residence of the imperial and royal minister for foreign affairs.

One of the courtyard's allegorical fountains

Map on pages 86–7

spring is surrounded by a pavilion built in 1779. The nymph statue is by Wilhelm Beyer, who was also responsible for the two **Naiad Fountains**.

THE GLORIETTE

Below: statues on the Gloriette colonnade
Bottom: the Tiergarten pavilion

Ascending the Schönbrunn Hill, you will finally reach the **★★ Gloriette**. The colonnade (1775, by Ferdinand von Hohenberg) was originally intended as a memorial to remind the imperial court, through its ancient funeral symbolism, of the fallen soldiers whose death had made peaceful court life possible. From here there is a stunning panorama over the city of Vienna. To the east of the Gloriette lies the **Little Gloriette**, with wall paintings by Nicolaus Paccassi.

At the foot of the Schönbrunn Hill lies the **★★ Tiergarten** (zoo). The zoo has been extensively modernised, providing large and interesting enclosures for the animals. Of the original buildings on this site, only the central pavilion (1752, by Jadot de Ville-Issey) remains as the café-restaurant. Highlights include a great new pool for the penguins, and new enclosures for the elephants and big cats. The aquarium is particularly impressive, with a spectacular coral reef and 'walk through' flooded Amazon rainforest.

Diagonally opposite is the parish church of Hietzing, dating from the 15th to 17th centuries.

THE WEST

The western outskirts of the city are well worth exploring, either to escape to the woods of the Lainzer Tiergarten, or to search out Otto Wagner's Jugendstil masterpiece at Vienna's exemplary psychiatric hospital.

To the south of the Schönbrunn is **Schloss Hetzendorf**, built in 1694 as a hunting lodge. The castle received its present appearance in 1743 and now houses the Vienna School of Fashion. It is the most attractive of the numerous little palaces dotted across the outer districts of the city. Of particular note are the interior staircases and the wall paintings (1746–7, by Daniel Gran) in the Great Hall and the chapel. The Fashion Museum displays some of the school's huge collection of clothing and accessories (open Tues–Sun 9am–noon).

Sprawling along the western boundary of the city is the **Lainzer Tiergarten** (Lainz Wildlife Park; open mid–Feb–mid-Nov: 8am–dusk, mid-Nov–mid-Feb: 9am–dusk: bus 60B from Speising). The park has a number of footpaths ranging from 2km (1 mile) to 12km (7½ miles) through its woods. Deer and wild boars roam freely, and wild horses, aurochs (European bisons) and moufflons (wild sheep) can be observed in enclosures. On the eastern edge of the forested area lies the **Hermesvilla** (1885; open Apr–Sept: Wed–Sun 10am–6pm, Oct–Mar: 9am–4.30pm), once a residence of Empress Elizabeth. The opulent villa, part of the Historisches Museum der Stadt Wien since 1978, is used to hold temporary exhibitions.

AM STEINHOF

The church ★★ **Am Steinhof**, located in the extensive grounds of the psychiatric hospital, is one of the crowning achievements of Viennese Art Nouveau. Built between 1904 and 1907 to a design by Otto Wagner, its unique character is underlined by its copper-clad dome and white marble cladding. The decorative sculptures are the work of Othmar Schumkowitz and Richard Luksch; the stained glass was designed by Kolo Moser (conducted tours: Sat 3pm: bus 48A from the Burgring).

Star Attractions
- Gloriette
- Tiergarten
- Am Steinhof

Technological Museum
Just to the north of the Schönbrunn, at Mariahilfer Strasse 212, is the newly renovated and child-friendly Technische Museum Wien (Technology Museum; open Mon–Sat 9am–6pm, Thur 9am–8pm, Sun 10am–6pm: www.tmw.ac.at).

Kolo Moser's windows in Am Steinhof

Map
on pages
86–7

DÖBLING

Döbling is one of the most attractive areas of the city. It falls into the outer metropolitan districts, but also marks the beginning of the Wienerwald (Vienna Woods) forests and vineyards. Most of the villages that now form the XIX district of the city can trace their origins back to the 11th and 12th centuries. From the reign of Maria Theresa, these former wine-growing villages were popular summer retreats for Viennese society.

Beethoven sites
Ludwig van Beethoven, who often stayed in Heiligenstadt, wrote his famous Heiligenstadt Testament, a bitter complaint about his incipient deafness, in the house at No 6 Probusgasse (museum) near St Michael's. The composer also stayed at No 2 Am Pfarrplatz. Memories of Beethoven are also awakened at No 26 Kahlenbergerstrasse and along the Beethovengang, which has a memorial to the composer dating from 1862.

GRINZING

The most famous district in Döbling is **Grinzing**. Mentioned in 1114 as 'Grinzingan', it is known as the archetypal *Heurige* village *(see page 114)*, and consequently overflows with tourists. Avoid establishments with coaches parked outside and look for the authentic ones, marked by a green Scots pine branch *(Buschen)* over the entrance.

Nestling between gardens and vineyards, the houses of Grinzing (16th and 17th centuries) are very picturesque, especially the Old House (Himmelstrasse 35). The onion tower of the Gothic parish church (1426, later rebuilt in the Baroque style) soars above the rooftops, and the old Trummelhof (Coblenzgasse 30) is said to have been built on the site of a Roman settlement, the ruins of which may explain the derivation of the name.

Döbling view over Leopoldberg and Vienna

SIEVERING

The Sieveringer Strasse winds through the straggling wine-growing village of **Sievering**, which was known as 'Siphringin' in 1156. In the centre stands the parish church (14th-century); on the south wall is a relief depicting the Mount of Olives (early 16th-century), and in the north aisle another (c. 1500) of the Nativity. The rest of the interior dates from the 18th century.

The oldest and most charming of Döbling's wine-growing villages is **Heiligenstadt** *(see box opposite)*. It is often mentioned in connection with St Severin (5th-century): a monastery which he founded here is said to have given the place the epithet *Locus sanctus*, the 'holy place', retained in the village's name to this day. Heiligenstadt's present-day appearance is largely characterised by Empire and Biedermeier houses, which can be seen in particular in the Armbrustergasse and along the Kahlenbergstrasse.

Sievering parish church

Where the Grinzing road and Hohe Warte intersect sits the parish church of St Michael (1894–8), a reconstruction of an earlier building. The 12th-century Romanesque church of St James is thought to stand on the site of Roman ruins.

NUSSDORF

Another ancient wine-growing village is **Nussdorf**. In the Greinergasse there are charming old houses and a Baroque parish church (1784–6).

Near the Nussdorfer Platz lies the Hackenhofergasse; No 17 houses the Zwettler Stiftshof, built in 1731 by Josef Munggenast, a pupil of Hildebrandt. Opposite (No 18) stands the Palais Schikaneder (1737), in which the librettist of Mozart's *Magic Flute*, Emanuel Schikaneder, lived from 1802 until 1807. At the beginning of the 20th century it became the home of Franz Lehár.

From the Nussdorfer Platz you can take the underpass under the Franz-Josefs-Bahn railway and continue to the Danube, alongside which runs a little promenade. The extensive locks of the Donaukanal, which begins here, were built between 1894 and 1898 by Otto Wagner.

Map on pages 86–7

THE HÖHENSTRASSE

Meandering along the northwestern borders of the city through the Vienna Woods is the **Höhenstrasse**. The road provides access to magnificent views of the city and the Danube. You can reach the Höhenstrasse via Salmannsdorf, Sievering or Grinzing; bus 38A runs from Heiligenstadt to Grinzing, to the Cobenzl observation point and the Kahlenberg. Near the car park there is a pretty footpath through woods, leading away from the Höhenstrasse, up to the summit of the Hermannskogel, the highest of the mountains on the northern boundary of Vienna (542m/1,778ft).

It was on the **Kahlenberg** (483m/1,585ft), previously known as the *Sauberg* because of the large numbers of wild boar living here, that Vienna's relief forces gathered during the Turkish siege of 1683. In the sacristy of the little church of St Joseph (1628), you will find memorials to King John Sobieski of Poland, the leader of the army. Beside the south side altar hangs a 14th-century copy of the *Black Madonna* of Tschenstochau.

A woodland path some 2km (1 mile) long leads to the **Leopoldsberg** (423m/1,388ft). The name recalls the Babenberg Duke Leopold III the Saintly, who in about 1100 built a castle here and made it his seat of government. The castle was destroyed by the Turks in 1529; the site, however, is marked by St Leopold's church (1718).

Höhenstrasse view
The panoramic view from the Leopoldsberg is similar to that from the Kahlenberg, stretching to the southeast from the Danube bridges and the Danube Park to the Prater. Behind, on the horizon, you can see the Leitha Mountains. Further to the right the built-up area of the city sprawls around St Stephen's Cathedral. In the south, behind Schönbrunn, can be seen the foothills of the Alps. To the west lies the Kahlenberg and in the north you can look down upon Klosterneuburg, behind which you can also make out Kreuzenstein Castle. To the northeast lie the plains of the Marchfeld, which extend as far as the Lesser Carpathians.

The Prater's Riesenrad

THE PRATER AND DANUBE

The **Prater**, an enormous area of parkland, lies east of the city centre across the Donaukanal, and extends southwards from the Praterstern. The visitor is likely to think in the first instance of the famous amusement park with its landmark ★ **Riesenrad** (big wheel), erected in 1897 by Walther Basset. It is the last remaining example of a series; Basset's giant wheels in London, Paris, Chicago and Blackpool have long since been dismantled. Vienna's giant wheel, famous in part for starring in *The Third Man*, takes you 64m (210ft) off the ground and offers a magnificent view of the city. Nearby is a station of the Liliputbahn miniature railway, which runs along the main avenue. The Prater also offers an enticing variety of merry-go-rounds, ghost trains, sideshows, etc.

The **Grüner Prater** is an extensive nature park with spacious meadows, clumps of trees and streams. The main avenue is almost 5km (3 miles) long and is bordered with chestnut trees which invite you to take leisurely walks. There are wine and beer taverns and cafés, plus the Lusthaus, a respectable establishment despite its name, built in 1782 by Isidor Canevale. For many centuries the Prater was reserved for members of the court and aristocracy. In 1766, Joseph II abolished these privileges and opened the park to the people of Vienna. The Prater is particularly attractive in May, when the chestnut trees are in flower.

THE TEGETTHOFF MONUMENT

Close to the Prater are two other sights of interest. The first of these is on Praterstern itself. The **Tegetthoff Monument** recalls the popular Austro-Hungarian Admiral Wilhelm von Tegetthoff, who was victorious over the Italian fleet at Lissa on the Adriatic in 1866. At Taborstrasse 16 is the **Kloster der barmherzigen Brüder**, founded in 1614 by Emperor Matthew. It acquired its present countenance between 1694–1748. Its Baroque interior is worth inspection, in particular the high altar with the fine painting *The Baptism of Christ* (1736) by Daniel Gran.

The Tegetthoff Monument

Map
on pages
86–7

UNO City

On the southern edge of the park lies UNO City, or the Vienna International Centre, built between 1973 and 1979 by Johann Staber *(see page 11)*, and the Austria Centre. UNO City houses the headquarters of various international bodies, such as the Atomic Energy Organisation and the High Commission for Refugees. Guided tours Mon–Fri 11am and 2pm; make sure you bring your passport.

The Vienna International Centre

ACROSS THE DANUBE

Until the 19th century the Danube divided into several branches as it flowed through Vienna. Several branches were very shallow, and frequent flooding made canalisation essential. Since then, the Danube has had only one branch, the Donaukanal; the **Alte Donau** (Old Danube) is now a lake with no link with the course of the river. Its green surroundings and 10-km (6-mile) long beach make it a paradise for bathers in summer. The largest island, the Gänsehäufel, is a popular bathing area.

The artificial **Donauinsel** (Donau island; 21km/13 miles long) lies on the Danube proper. Known to the Viennese as Copa Cagrana after the nearby suburb of Kagran, this is the city's favourite recreation and leisure area. Ideal for sunbathing, there are nudist areas in the north and south. Sports facilities include rowing, paddle boating, sailing, cycling and swimming.

Between Alte and Neue Donau is **Donaupark**. The Donauturm (Danube Tower; 252m/827ft) here has a terrace at a height of 150m (492ft) with a magnificent view over the city. An even better panorama can be surveyed from the revolving café-restaurant at 165m (541ft).

Further south along the left bank of the Danube is **Lobau**. The rural character of the Lobau recalls the Alte Donau area. The landscape, with watercourses, marshes and lakes, is almost untouched.

VIENNESE CEMETERIES

Given the alleged Viennese preoccupation with death *(see page 11)*, it is fitting that Vienna should have suitably impressive cemeteries, on a par with those of Paris.

The ★ **Zentralfriedhof** (Central Cemetery) is the largest in the country (some 243 hectares/600 acres), and was laid out in 1874. The graves of many famous people can be found near the second gate, including the composers Cristoph Willibald Gluck (1714–87), Ludwig van Beethoven (1770–1827), Franz Schubert (1797–1828), Josef Lanner (1801–43), Johann Strauss the Elder (1804–49), Johann Strauss the Younger (1825–99), Johannes Brahms (1833–97), Hugo Wolf (1860–1903) and Arnold Schoenberg (1874–1951). Also here are the poets Johann Nestroy (1801–62), Ludwig Anzengruber (1839–89) and Anton Wildgans (1881–1932); and the actors Hans Moser (1880–1964), Theo Lingen (1903–79) and Curt Jürgens (1915–82). Visual artists include the sculptors Viktor Tilgner (1844–96) and Fritz Wotruba (1907–75). The former Chancellor of the Federal Republic, Bruno Kreisky (1911–90), is also here. In the Jewish section near Gate 1 are the writers Karl Kraus (1874–1936) and Artur Schnitzler (1862–1931).

Beethoven's grave in the Zentralfriedhof

MORE FAMOUS GRAVES

Mozart (1756–91) was buried in a pauper's grave in **St Marxer Friedhof** (Leberstrasse 6–8), Vienna's last Biedermeier cemetery. The exact spot is not known; a mourning angel leaning against a pillar marks the supposed site.

Hietzinger Friedhof (on Maxingstrasse) has the graves of poet Franz Grillparzer (1791–1872) and composer Alban Berg (1885–1935), while **Kalksburger Friedhof** (on Josef-Weber-Strasse) has the grave of poet Hugo von Hofmannsthal (1874–1929), who lived for many years in Ridaun (in 'Schloss Hofmannsthal', on Ketzergasse).

Grinzinger Friedhof, on An den langen Lüssen, is where the famous Viennese composer Gustav Mahler (1860–1911) is buried.

Map
on pages
86–7

Wachau
The romantic Danube Valley of the ★ Wachau to the west of Vienna and its little towns of Krems, Dürnstein, Spitz, Ybbs and Melk (the famous 18th-century abbey) can be visited as a day-trip from the capital.

Klosterneuburg abbey

Further Afield

Klosterneuburg in Lower Austria is 13km (8 miles) north of Vienna. The town, which lies on the Danube, is named after the famous Augustinian abbey founded in 1133 by Leopold III. The abbey church boasts the magnificent Verdun Altar dating from 1181; the monastery includes imperial apartments.

★ **Carnuntum** lies 42km (26 miles) east of Vienna, near Petronell. The ruins of the largest Roman garrison in Austria include two amphitheatres, a Heathens' Gateway, and the Museum Carnuntium in Bad Deutsch-Altenburg. About 10km (6 miles) further east lies the town of Hainburg, still surrounded by its 13th-centry city walls. From Bad Deutsch-Altenburg it is not far to Prellenkirchen, where you will find one of the prettiest streets of wine-tasting cellars in the country. One or two of them are always open during the summer months.

Laxenburg lies 15km (9 miles) south of Vienna. The park surrounding the former imperial summer residence (1693) with its grottoes, waterfalls and the moated castle, the Franzensburg, built in 1801, are worth a visit.

SOUTHERN WIENERWALD

Also worth visiting is the **Southern Wienerwald**. This takes in the 12th-century Liechtenstein Castle near Brunn and the Lake Grotto near Mödling (for a boat trip on an underground lake). Passing by the Höldrichsmühle, the mill where Franz Schubert is said to have composed his famous song 'Der Lindenbaum' from *Winterreise*, you will arrive at the famous Cistercian Abbey of Heiligenkreuz (1135) and the hunting lodge at Mayerling. This is where the tragic Crown Prince Rudolf shot first his mistress Mary Vetsera and then himself, in 1889.

Past the delightful Helenental you will reach Baden, whose famous mineral springs were known in Roman times, before returning to Vienna via the famous wine-growing area of Gumpoldskirchen, with its Renaissance town hall, built in 1559.

Semmering lies 110km (68 miles) to the south of Vienna. The magnificent mountain and forest scenery afford plenty of scope for walking.

THE BURGENLAND

The Burgenland to the southeast of Vienna is the setting for the largest steppe-type lake in Europe, **Lake Neusiedler** (320sq km/123sq miles). The main villages on the lake are Podersdorf and Neusiedl, as well as the festival town of Mörbisch, and Rust, the town famous for its storks' nests.

To the east of the lake extends the Seewinkel, which marks the beginning of the Puszta, the Hungarian lowland plains. Illmitz nestles peacefully in the middle of a large nature reserve with a number of rare animal and plant species.

EISENSTADT

The capital of the Burgenland is **Eisenstadt** (70km/43 miles from Vienna). Josef Haydn lived and composed here for many years in Esterházy Castle; he is buried in the Bergkirche (Church of the Calvary). Popular excursion destinations in the Burgenland are the large quarry, St Margarethen (an open-air museum with modern sculpture and passion plays), the crystal-clear Lake Neufelder and Forchenstein Castle (c. 1300).

Below: Mödling church pulpit
Bottom: a Burgenland vine

Art and Architecture

Although there has been a settlement on the site of central Vienna since around 400 BC, the officers' quarters excavated under the Hoher Markt are all that remain today to give an impression of the Roman town, Vindobona. The ground plan of Ruprechtskirche, with its semi-circular apse pointing towards the Graben (the walls of the military camp), may also date from late-Roman times.

ROMANESQUE AND GOTHIC

As with earlier periods, hardly anything remains of Vienna under the Babenbergs (who ruled Austria from around 976 until 1248). Their basilica-like Romanesque buildings have disappeared almost without trace. Some sections of Ruprechtskirche and the parish church in Heiligenstadt are thought to date from the 11th century; and the original building of Stephansdom dates from the first half of the 12th century. The construction of Maria am Gestade and the Schottenkirche must have commenced at around the same time.

The second stages of the Schottenkirche and Stephansdom date from the 13th century and, despite later rebuilding, the Schottenkirche gives the impression of a late-Romanesque cruciform basilica, whilst the massive walls of the west facade of Stephansdom, and its twin Heidentürme (Towers of the Pagans), display Gothic elements.

Towards the end of the 13th century, under the influence of the mendicant monastic orders, the Gothic style became established in Vienna as elsewhere in Europe. The squat buildings of the Romanesque era were replaced by high, light-filled buildings whose vaulted roofs and pointed arches were supported by slender columns and buttresses. During the second half of the 14th century, the ruling class began to have an active influence on the construction of religious buildings.

The impressive Gothic nave of Stephansdom is an expression of the magnificence of the court of the time and of the desire to see Vienna elevated to the rank of bishopric.

The Renaissance
The Italian Renaissance made little impression on the city and is only represented by the arcaded courtyards in the noblemen's mansions (the Stallburg) and the merchants' houses (Bäckerstrasse 7), and by the magnificently decorated gate leading into the Schweitzerhof of the palace.

*Opposite: the exterior of the Stephansdom Gothic nave
Below: modern stained glass, Ruprechtskirche*

THE BAROQUE

Vienna's architectural Golden Age began after 1683. The Baroque style became the city's most characteristic architectural form, acquiring as it did so an individual note. The Jesuit style of Andrea Pozzo, and the magnificence of Burnacini and the Carlone and d'Allio families, were gradually supplanted by local master builders who developed and perfected the Austrian Baroque style; Johann Bernhard Fischer von Erlach and his main rival, Lukas von Hildebrandt. Outstanding among the many masterpieces of the era are the works of Fischer von Erlach's son Josef Emanuel, who was primarily responsible for the posthumous completion of his father's designs, and whose style already heralds the Classicism that was to follow. Particularly noteworthy examples of Viennese Baroque include: the row of palaces along Herrengasse; the interior of the Nationalbibliothek; the Oberes Belvedere; and Karlskirche.

Below: the magnificent trompe l'oeil Baroque ceiling of the Jesuitenkirche
Bottom: Otto Wagner's Karlsplatz U-Bahn pavilion

In Vienna, the Rococo style was largely restricted to internal decoration. Inspired by the philosophy of the Enlightenment, the Baroque age was succeeded by the simplicity of Classicism (from c. 1770). At the same time, Vienna developed an architectural style of its own, the Biedermeier, a form of domestic Classicism, which lent middle class homes their characteristic restrained appearance.

KARLSPLATZ

THE RINGSTRASSE AND SECESSION

In the middle of the 19th century, following the demolition of the old city walls, a new building phase began along the course of the Ringstrasse. The prominent style borrowed from different architectural movements and became known as the Historical or Historic Revival style. Also known as the Ringstrasse style, it became the dominant architectural form of the era. Architects such as Theophil Hansen and Heinrich Ferstel were responsible for huge official and public buildings such as the Parlament, Börse and Burgtheater.

It was succeeded in around 1900 by the Secessionist (Jugendstil or Art Nouveau) architecture of men such as Otto Wagner *(see box)* and Joseph Maria Olbrich. Inspired by a break from the conservative Akademie der Bildenden Künste, the style is characterised by clean, almost Modernist lines, and restrained, elegant decoration.

The Secession was itself replaced only a decade later by the New Functionalism of Adolf Loos, whose Loos Haus on Michaelerplatz created such a stir when it was built in 1909–11 *(see page 38)*. His flat-roofed and symmetrical Steiner Haus (1910) was the first domestic Modernist building.

> **Otto Wagner**
> One of the seminal architects of the early-20th century, Wagner (1841–1918) was almost single-handedly responsible for the move away from Ringstrasse Historicism, towards the first glimmering of modern architecture exemplified by the Jugendstil. His most important buildings include, the Postsparkasse *(see page 59)*, Am Steinhof *(see page 93)* and his numerous works for Vienna's U-Bahn.

CONTEMPORARY ARCHITECTURE

For a city apparently so much in thrall to its past, Vienna has a surprising amount of excellent contemporary architecture. The post-First World War Social Democratic experiments in social housing, exemplified by the huge Karl-Marx-Hof on Heiligenstädterstrasse, were disrupted by the onset of Nazi rule, and the city didn't recover its experimental edge until the 1980s.

Hans Hollein's Haas Haus *(see page 22)* acted as a catalyst, and since then, encouraged by progressive city administrations, architects have set about transforming the city. Subsequent projects, such as Ortner and Ortner's MuseumsQuartier *(see page 77)* and the startling conversion of Simmering's gasometers into residences (in part by the inventive and influential Coop-Himmelblau), have greatly added to Vienna's cityscape.

Lucretia *by Lucas Cranach the Elder*

SCULPTURE AND PAINTING

Unfortunately the only substantial example of Viennese Romanesque sculpture is to be seen on the Riesentor of Stephansdom. However, there are many fine examples of Gothic sculpture, particularly the stone figures adorning the exterior and interior of Stephansdom. The magnificent baldachin statues in the nave, Gerhaert van Leyden's massive tomb for Emperor Frederick II and Anton Pilgram's pulpit with its entwined branches and vines, all represent unsurpassed examples of Gothic decorative skills.

Other famous examples include the main door of the Minoritenkirche by Jacques de Paris, the decorative pillar *Spinnerin am Kreuz* by Hans Puchsbaum and the triple portrait of the patron saint in the Annakirche by Veit Stoss.

Gothic panel painting, which assumed a dominant role in the Vienna of the 14th century, also provides the earliest example of German portraiture in the painting of Rudolf IV (c. 1360), ascribed to Heinrich Vaschang. A predilection for natural landscape painting can be seen clearly in the Madonna Cycle (c. 1470) by the Master of the Scottish Altar, to whom we also owe the earliest panorama of the city of Vienna.

Shortly before 1500, the Danube School of Painting developed in the Vienna region. The artists who followed this style combined landscape painting with the expression of deep emotion and imagination; the main representative, Lucas Cranach the Elder, worked in Vienna 1500–2.

BAROQUE PAINTING

During the Baroque, many sumptuous rooms were decorated with magnificent frescoes, a number of which were painted by the Austrian artists Johann Michael Rottmayr and Daniel Gran. The influential Baroque painter Paul Troger also worked in Vienna. Other artists included Martino Altomonte, Carlo Carlone and Gregorio Guglielmi. The later works of Franz Anton Maulpertsch and Johann Martin Schmidt represent the peak of the High Baroque in Viennese painting.

Lomography
One of the more bizarre artistic movements that has originated in Vienna is Lomography. Inspired by the strangely distorted pictures taken by the Russian-built Lomo cameras, two Viennese students, Matthias Fiegl and Wolfgang Stranziger, began to mount exhibitions in the early 1990s. Since then the art of Lomography has become an international movement. For more information see www.lomography.com

The Kiss *by Gustav Klimt*

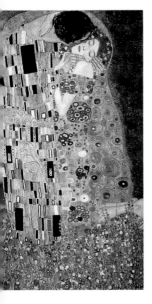

19TH- AND 20TH-CENTURY ART

The suppression of public dissent and political activity in Austria after the Napoleonic wars had a great impact on the arts. Painting of the Biedermeier period was solidly bourgeois, concentrating on idealised and sentimental rural scenes and family portraits. Painters active during this time include Josef Führich and Moritz von Schwind (allegories and mythological subjects), Michael Daffinger (miniatures), and Jacob and Rudolf von Alt (landscapes).

Towards the end of the 19th century, the 'Ringstrasse' era, painting came to be dominated by Historicist themes, in particular by Karl Rahl, Hans Canon and, amongst others, Hans Makart. However, other painters were open to the influence of the French Impressionists, including Tina Blau-Lang and Theodor von Hörmann.

Their work was admired by painters of the Secession, of which the most famous representative is Gustav Klimt. This Viennese Art Nouveau laid the foundations for the Expressionism of Egon Schiele and Oskar Kokoschka.

During the later 20th century, perhaps the most significant Viennese artists were the 1960s Actionists *(see page 77)* and, locally at least, Friedensreich Hundertwasser *(see page 59)*. The most high-profile contemporary sculptors are Fritz Wotruba and Alfred Hrdlicka.

Below: Rodin's bust of Gustav Mahler
Bottom: the eponymous statue on Beethovenplatz

Music

Vienna's place in the history of Western art music is unrivalled by almost any other city. The 'Golden Age of the Minnesang' at the beginning of the 13th century, when Kürnberger, Walther von der Vogelweide, Neidhart von Reuenthal and Thannhäuser were at the Viennese court, marked the start of this passion for music. However, for the next 300 years or so, music was closely associated with the court. The performance of opera in particular – like *Il Pomo d'Oro* (by Antonio Cesti, 1666), with costs amounting to 100,000 guilders – remained the prerogative of the emperor.

Johann Josef Fux, the 'Austrian Palestrina', began to break free from the influence of Italy at the end of the 17th and beginning of the 18th century. Later, from 1748, Christoph Willibald Gluck took up residence in Vienna and broke the Italian monopoly on the operatic stage.

THE CLASSICAL ERA

From the reign of Maria Theresa onwards, the patronage of music extended from the emperor himself to the nobility. Joseph Haydn, Wolfgang Amadeus Mozart and Ludwig van Beethoven, the outstanding trio of the Classical composers, were all resident in Vienna for significant portions of

The Vienna Philharmonic
This internationally acclaimed orchestra was founded in 1841 by Otto Nicolai and Nikolaus Lenau. It consists solely of members of the Vienna State Opera Orchestra. Past conductors at the Staatsoper have included Gustav Mahler, who turned the orchestra into a world class ensemble. Since 1908 the players have chosen their own permanent conductor, including such illustrious musicians as Wilhelm Furtwängler, who led the orchestra from 1928 to 1954.

The Griechenbeisl, famous for Viennese song

their lives. Franz Schubert, who represents the transition from musical Classicism to Romanticism, was born in the city. He marked the beginning of the German lieder tradition with his setting of Goethe's poem, the *Erlkönig* (1816).

ROMANTICISM AND THE 20TH CENTURY

In second half of the 19th century, Vienna saw Anton Bruckner compose his powerful symphonies, Hugo Wolf writing *Lieder*, and Johannes Brahms, a native of Hamburg, set up his new home in the city. Franz von Suppé, Karl Millöcker, Michael Ziehrer, Franz Lehár and Leo Fall were all composing operettas, a Viennese tradition which Robert Stolz continued.

The modern musical age dawned in the early-20th century with the compositions of Gustav Mahler and Richard Strauss. Their post-Romantic vision was carried on by Wilhelm Kienzl, Erich Korngold and Franz Schmidt. Arnold Schoenberg, while intially steeped in post-Romanticism, soon took its ideas to their logical conclusion and began exploring the world of atonality. Along with his students Anton Webern and Alban Berg, he then went on to develop and codify these ideas into 12-tone composition.

Contemporary composers with strong associations with Vienna include György Ligeti, Friedrich Cerha, Ernst Krenek, HK Gruber and, most recently, Olga Neuwirth.

A decorative panel in the Sala Terrena, Vienna's oldest concert hall

THE VIENNESE WALTZ

This musical dance form was reputedly introduced by Neidhart von Reuenthal in about 1230. However, it is generally held that the waltz, whose name occurs for the first time during the 18th century, developed from the rustic *Ländler* in slow 3/4 time. At the beginning of the 19th century, the tempo of the waltz was progressively tightened, and it became the most popular dance form amongst the middle classes. Josef Lanner, together with Johann Strauss (both father and son), gave the dance its classic form.

HEURIGENMUSIK

During the 19th century, the brothers Johann and Josef Schrammel were performing in *Heurige* what came to be known as *Schrammelmusik*. This music developed from the violin melodies played for dances, and from old ballads. Whilst in Johann Schrammel's days, Heurigenmusik was mostly played by a quartet of musicians (two violins, guitar and clarinet), today it is usually performed by a trio consisting of violin, guitar and accordion.

Viennese songs

The first book of Viennese songs was published in 1686, the period of the legendary Augustin Mitte *(see page 57)*. However, the 'Golden Age' of Viennese song was during the 19th and early 20th century, when it was encouraged by performances in the *Heurigen*. Many of these songs, such as *Wien, Wien, nur du allein* (Vienna, Vienna, only you...) and *Mei Mutterl war a Weanerin* (My Mother was Viennese...), are still popular today.

The Burgtheater on the Ringstrasse

WIENER SÄNGERKNABEN

The famous, if somewhat overhyped, Wiener Sängerknaben (or Vienna Boys' Choir), was founded in 1498 as part of the Imperial chapel choir with 16 to 20 choir boys. It increased steadily in size over the years, and in the 18th and 19th centuries included Josef Haydn and Franz Schubert among its members. Re-established in 1924, it today consists of four individual choirs, each having 24 members.

The Wiener Sängerknaben sings Mass on Sunday and church festivals in the Burgkapelle *(see page 42)* for which tickets must be booked in advance. They also sing occasional mixed programmes of motets, madrigals, waltz music and folk songs in the Musikverein. See their website www.wsk.at, or tel: 216 3942, for further information.

Literature and Theatre

By contrast with the richness of Austrian medieval poetry, the 14th to 17th centuries produced little of significance. Following that period, representatives of popular folk literature include Stranitzky's dramatic hero *Hanswurst* (from 1705) and Carl Laroche's *Kasperl* (from 1787).

Vienna became prominent once more with the famous and influential playwright, Franz Grillparzer (1791–1872). In his dramas, such as *Family Strife in Habsburg*, *A Dream is Life* and *Woe to Him who Lies!*, he strove to comment on the human condition while avoiding the approbrium of the state censors. At the same time, the Viennese theatre acquired its characteristic lightheartedness from Ferdinand Raimund, and from Johann Nestroy its often biting wit *(Lumpazivagabundus)*.

The playwright Franz Grillparzer

At the end of the 19th century, Vienna saw the development of pyschoanalysis, the impact of which can be seen in the writing of Arthur Schnitzler (1862–1921). A friend of Freud and member of the *Junge Wien* (Young Vienna) group of writers, he is best known for *Dream Story* (1926) and his play *Riegen* (1900).

Four writers associated with the *Junge Wien* are Hugo von Hofmannsthal (1874–1929), Hermann Bahr (1863–1934), Peter Altenberg (1859–1919), and Karl Kraus (1874–1936). Hofmannsthal is perhaps best known for his librettos for the operas of Richard Strauss, while Kraus is remembered for his biting satire. Two other writers active at the time are Georg Trakl (1887–1914) and Joseph Roth (1894–1939); both famous for their angst-ridden lives. Trakl is known for his intensely miserable and introspective poety. Roth, although he was not born in Vienna and died in Paris, set his books during the last years of the Hapsburgs.

Later Viennese writers include: Robert Musil (1880–1942), remembered for his huge, and unfinished, *Man Without Qualities*; the tragic but hugely talented Jewish writer, Stefan Zweig (1881–1942), who fled from the Nazis only to commit suicide in Brazil; and Thomas Bernhard (1931–89), best known for his book *Wittgenstein's Nephew*.

FOOD AND DRINK

The cuisine of Vienna has long enjoyed an excellent reputation on account of its variety and refinement. For centuries it has been enriched by dishes from Hungary, Bohemia, Italy and France, and more recently by specialities from the Alpine regions.

The beef dishes are particularly good. The Viennese often simmer meat for long periods as Tafelspitz (a particular cut of beef). Also popular is Rostbraten (rib of beef, usually roast with onions) and goulash, made with beef or veal. Another speciality is the crisply coated Wiener Schnitzel, which is made with veal.

Fish dishes usually include carp (which in Vienna is mostly baked), or – more frequently – Fogosch (pike or perch), grilled and served with sauce tartare. Some restaurants also serve trout (usually 'blue'). The favourite poultry dish is deep-fried chicken, which is a long-standing Viennese speciality.

However, Vienna is particularly famous for its puddings. The most common amongst these are Strudel of all kinds (thin pastry with a variety of fillings); apple, cream and quark Strudel are very popular, as is Schmarrn (baked pancake cut into small pieces and served with a variety of fillings). The famous Sachertorte was invented in 1832 by Prince Metternich's chef, Franz Sacher. Its ingredients include egg yolks, melted chocolate, almonds, a small quantity of flour, sugar and whisked egg whites; it is covered with apricot jam and a layer of chocolate icing. A Sachertorte keeps well for several weeks.

Opposite: Wiener Schnitzel as served at Figlmüller

WINE AND BEER

The best local wines come from the Vienna Woods (Grinzinger, Klosterneuburger, Nussberger, Gumpoldskirchner, Pfaffstättner), or Kremser, Loibner, Dürnsteiner from the Wachau. Northern Lower Austria produces the piquant, crisp wines Retzer, Haugsdorfer, Mailberger and Matzener. Ask for a *viertel* (⅛ litre) or an *achtel* (¼ litre).

A few Viennese dishes
Backerbsen crisp dough balls served in soup
Bauernschmaus a variety of meats served with sausages, sauerkraut and dumplings
Beinfleisch boiled beef
Beuschl lung, heart and spleen of veal, prepared in vinegar
Buchteln filled, oven-baked dumplings
Faschiertes mincemeat
Fischbeuschlsuppe vegetable soup with fish roe
Fisolen French beans
Frittaten strips of pancake, served in soup
Geröstete fried potatoes
Geselchtes smoked meat
Gugelhupf a type of sponge cake
Häuptesalat green salad
Kaiserfleisch smoked belly of pork
Karfiol cauliflower
Kipferl croissant
Krenfleisch suckling pig boiled with crackling
Lungenbraten loin of beef in cream sauce
Lungenstrudel pastry filled with offal, served in soup
Marillenknödel apricot dumplings
Palatschinken filled pancake
Rahm sour cream
Schlagobers whipped cream
Stelze knuckle of pork or veal
Tiroler Knödel ham dumplings
Topfen a type of curd cheese

Apart from the well-known Viennese beers (Liesinger, Ottakringer and Schwechater), another popular brew is Gösser Bier from Styria. Draught beer is ordered as a *Seidl* (⅓ litre) or *Krügl* (½ litre).

HEURIGE

The word *Heuriger* – an Austrian term for wine of the latest vintage – is changed to Heurige when it refers to the vintner's pub in which this new wine is served. The tradition goes back over eight hundred years: in the 12th century, locally produced wines were served in the city centre in the so-called Lucken. After the Turkish sieges this practice was to a large extent transferred to the suburbs.

Authentic Heurige can be recognised by unpretentious furnishings (the landlords are vintners, not interior designers), simple but excellent self-service buffets, by a Scots pine branch (Bushen) hung on a pole above the door, indicating that wines are being served, by the proud claim 'our own vintage', and by modest prices.

Vegetarian options

Vegetarians are in for a hard time in Vienna. However, things are changing, slowly, and the restaurants below are good for an escape from meat-dominated menus.

Art of Life, Stubenring 14, tel: 512 5553. Vegetarian and fish dishes with an East Asian twist. It also has a no smoking section. €€

Siddhartha, Fleischmarkt 16, tel: 513 1197. Well-established, serving dishes with a Viennese take on Indian and Nepalese food. €€

Vegie, Naschmarkt 232–4, tel: 586 6607. Tasty East Asian dishes, including home-made noodles, rice and tofu. Daily specials. €€

Wrenkh, Bauernmarkt 10, tel: 533 1526. A café and restaurant with Vienna's best vegetarian food. Salads and fresh vegetables served up in a cool, modern interior. €–€€

If you want to visit an authentic Heurige, your best plan is to avoid organised tours and set off independently. It's easy to find the most famous establishments in Grinzing *(see page 94)*, but many of these are very much geared to the tourist market. However, you can find good traditional addresses in Strebersdorf, Stammersdorf, Jedlersdorf, Ottakring or Sievering; or in one of the villages in the Vienna Woods.

Where to Eat

The following are recommended restaurants in the city. They are listed according to three categories: **€€€** = expensive; **€€** = moderate; **€** = cheap.

€€€

Altwienerhof, Herklotzgasse 6, tel: 8922 6000. Out in district XV, Altwienerhof serves very expensive, but delicious, French-influenced dishes.

Drei Husaren, Weihburggasse 4, tel: 512 1092. For genuine gut-busting Viennese fare, this, one of the city's oldest restaurants, is the place to go.

Hummerbar Fischrestaurant Kervansaray, Mahlerstrasse 9, tel: 512 8843. Fish and seafood dishes, particularly lobster, are the speciality in this excellent Turkish restaurant.

Korso, Mahlerstrasse 2, tel: 5151 6546. Korso, located in the Hotel Bristol, produces wonderful classic Viennese meat and fish dishes, and sumptuous desserts.

Palais Schwarzenberg, Schwarzenbergplatz 9, tel: 798 4515. Rich Viennese food in the opulent surroundings of the Hotel Palais Schwarzenberg.

Steirereck, Rasumovskygasse 2, tel: 713 3168. Considered by many Viennese to be the finest restaurant in the city. Predominantly Austrian cooking, with a good wine list and a great selection of cheeses.

€€

Aioli, Stephansplatz 12, tel: 532 0373. A Mediterranean restaurant on the third floor of the Haas Haus, serving excellent tapas and antipasti.

Beim Czaak, Postgasse 15, tel: 513 7215. A friendly *Beisl* (bistro) with helpful staff. Great food, particularly the Tafelspitz, and sinful desserts.

Figlmüller, Wollzeile 5, tel: 512 6177. This Stadtheurigen (city pub) is justly famed for the size and quality of its *Wiener Schnitzel*. However, it is a little expensive and touristy.

Griechenbeisl, Fleischmarkt 11, tel: 533 1941. A comfy, wood-pannelled cellar. Reasonable food and attentive staff *(see also page 57)*.

Livingstone, Zelinkagasse 4, tel: 533 3393. Well-prepared, Pacific rim-inspired food. Popular with young Viennese, so booking is advised.

MAK Café, Stubenring 5, tel: 714 0121. Beautifully designed café/restaurant with a garden for summer eating. Well-executed modern Viennese dishes with a couple of vegetarian options. No credit cards.

Neu Wien, Bäckerstrasse 5, tel: 512 0999. Very good modern Viennese cooking. The minimalist setting is decorated with contemporary art. Credit-card fraud has been reported, so it is safer to pay in cash.

€

Esterhazy Keller, Haarhof 1, tel: 533 3482. A Stadtheurigen in a dark cellar; fine and atmospheric in a very Viennese sort of way.

Nordsee, Kärntner Strasse 25, tel: 512 7354. The most central of a chain of fast-food fish restaurants. Good-value salads, sandwiches and hot dishes. Also on Kohlmarkt and Naschmarkt.

Trześniewski, Dorotheergasse 1, tel: 512 3291. One of a chain of stand-and-eat sandwich and snack bars. Very cheap, tasty and filling. Also on Mariahilferstrasse.

Zwölf Apostelkeller, Sonnenfelsgasse 3, tel: 512 6777. A large and popular Stadtheurigen cellar with a laid-back atmosphere, named after its 17th-century clock crowned with cast figures of the apostles.

CAFES

Within a few years of the founding of the first coffee house in 1683 by a Pole called Kolschitzky, the Viennese café had become the focal point of social life in the city; a role it continues to play today. During the Biedermeier period in particular, a Viennese café was luxuriously furnished with velvet

*The plush surroundings
of Café Diglas*

upholstery and silver tableware. Then as now, the guest could read the newspaper or play billiards or cards; the waiter will automatically refill the glass of water served with each cup of coffee. Vienna's cafés also serve food and, of course, delicious pastries.

Central, Herrengasse 14. Has a nice mock-Gothic vaulted ceiling, worth a visit even if touristy. No smoking area near the door *(see also page 49)*.

Demel, Kohlmarkt 14. A candidate for providing Vienna's best cakes, Demel has an elegant gilded and mirrored interior, and a no smoking area.

Diglas, Wollzeile 10. One of the very best; the cosy velvet seats and excellent cakes mean that once ensconced it is very difficult to leave.

Do&Co, Stephansplatz 12. Looking out over Stephansdom from its vantage point in the Haas Haus, this is one of Vienna's trendier cafés.

Frauenhuber, Himmelpfortgasse 1. Vienna's oldest extant café (founded in 1788), allegedly the scene of performances by Mozart and Beethoven.

Hawelka , Dorotheergasse 6. Legends in their own lifetime, the husband and wife who run the café work hard to cultivate its bohemian feel.

Coffee lexicon

Einspänner black coffee in a glass with whipped cream

Fiaker black coffee with rum

Kapuzine small coffee with a drop of cream

Kleiner/Grosser Brauner small/large white coffee

Kleiner/Grosser Mokka small/large black coffee

Melange large milky coffee

Mokka gespritzt black coffee with cognac

Piccolo small black coffee with/without whipped cream

Schlagobers whipped cream

Imperial, Kärntner Ring 16. Very swish and sedate in the Hotel Imperial, with a no smoking section at the back. Lovely hot chocolate.

Landtmann, Dr Karl-Lueger-Ring 4. A patrician café full of business people, but comfortable and accommodating nonetheless.

Palmenhaus, Burggarten. A popular café set in the great location of a Jugendstil glasshouse and with a tasteful modern design.

Prückl, Stubenring 24. A wonderful period interior and good selection of cakes and newspapers make this a good place to while away the hours.

Schwarzenberg, Kärtnerring 17. A traditional Ringstrasse café, complete with aloof waiters and a Jugendstil interior. Also has a no smoking area.

Nightlife

Vienna's nightlife has, in the past, tended to concentrate on the not-inconsiderable charms of its restaurants, cafés and live classical music venues. While these still remain, there are now plenty of decent clubs and venues playing dance music; many with resident DJs.

As everywhere, the scene changes quickly and it is best to find out the latest information on the ground (check out the German-only websites www.falter.at and www.city2002.at). Record shops are also a good source of information.

The 'in' places used to be found in the so-called 'Bermuda Triangle' around St Rupert's Church. This is no longer the case; the clubs here are generally staid and old hat.

Other areas that are more promising include the district around Bäckerstrasse, at the Rudolfsplatz and outside the city centre on the Spittelberg. During the summer there are many outdoor events, generally along the banks of the Danube.

SHOPPING

MARKETS

Those in search of a bargain piece of furniture or knick-knacks might try the Vienna flea market, or *Flohmarkt*, on Kettenbrückengasse (Sat until 5pm). Vienna's largest daily market is the Naschmarkt. This is a good place to find Austrian specialities, sold on the numerous farmer's stalls.

ANTIQUES

Few cities have as many antique shops; many are clustered around the Dorotheum (Dorotheergasse 17), the largest auction house in Europe. Other areas which have a concentration of antique and junk shops are near to Siebensterngasse and Josefstädter-strasse.

BOOKS AND CDS

Amadeus, at Mariahilferstrasse 99, is one of Vienna's best general book-shops. For travel guides and maps, Freytag & Berndt (Kohlmarkt 9) is the best place to head for. Books and mag-azines in English can be found at Shakespeare & Co (Sterngasse 2), and in the British Bookshop (Weih-burggasse 24). One of the best places for classical CDs is the Virgin Mega-store (Mariahilferstrasse 37–9).

CAKES & CONFECTIONERY

Vienna's famous Sachertorte can be obtained from Hotel Sacher, and its 'competitors', along with beautifully packaged confectionery, at Demel. Imperial-Torte (Emperor Cake) is on sale at the Bristol and Imperial Hotels; the triangular Domspitz can be found at the Do & Co Café. Some of the best patisserie cames from long-estab-lished Gerstner (Kärntnerstrasse 15) and Heiner (Kärntnerstrasse 21 and Wollzeile 9).

INTERIOR DESIGN

Lobmeyr (Kärntnerstrasse 26) stocks glass design ranging from Josef Hoff-mann to Matteo Thun. Augarten, the former imperial porcelain manufac-turers, can be found at the corner of Graben and Seilergasse. Thornet, famed for their bentwood chairs and Wiener Werkstätte furniture, is at Bergasse 31. Woka, at Singerstrasse 16, produce copies of Wiener Werk-stätte and Loos lamps and lighting.

JEWELLERY

Graben and the Kohlmarkt are where the city's established jewellery firms are based, some of which still proudly use the old imperial prefix k.u.k. Hoflieferant ('by appointment to the court').

Fashion

Most famous international names (for example Chanel, Max Mara and Missoni) can be found on or around Kärntner-strasse and Graben. Vienna's answer to Harvey Nichols is the huge fashion department store Steffl at Kärntnerstrasse 19. Austria's most famous international designer, Helmut Lang, has his shop at Seilergasse 6.

For lingerie, the Austrian chain Palmers has numerous branches in the city centre, or, at the the luxury end of the market, La Perla can be found on Albertinaplatz. The Austrian firm Wol-ford, famous for its tights and stockings, has a branch, among others, at Kärtnerstrasse 29.

If you are looking for handmade shoes, check out the shops of designer Ludwig Reiter; his flagship store is in the Dreimmäderlhaus, Mölkersteig 1.

Traditional Austrian dress, *Tracht* and *Loden*, can be found at Loden-Planck at Michaelerplatz 6. Fine Austrian knitware is available from Dr Haider-Petkov, Kohlmarkt 11.

PRACTICAL INFORMATION

Getting There

BY AIR

Austrian Airlines (www.aua.com) operates scheduled services to Vienna from London Heathrow. British Airways flies direct from both Heathrow and Gatwick, and Lauda-Air has a direct service from Gatwick. The no-frills airline Ryanair (www.ryanair.com) flies from London Stanstead to Salzburg, from where you can take the very reliable and regular train service to Vienna (circa 3 hours).

Vienna Schwechat airport is 19km (12 miles) from the city centre (arrivals, tel: 7007 22197; departures, tel: 7007 22184). Every 20 minutes between 6.30am and 11.30pm (every 30 minutes 11.30pm–6.30am), express buses provide a direct link with the City Air Terminal (Wien Mitte) on Landstrasse (approximately 15 minutes), from where there are convenient connections with all parts of the city via underground (U-Bahn) or suburban railway (S-Bahn).

There is also a shuttle service providing minibus transport direct to the various hotels, which can be reserved when you book your hotel accommodation or at Schwechat airport.

Between 7.30am and 8.30pm there is also an hourly S-Bahn connection (line S7) to Wien Mitte (the City Air Terminal). This journey from the airport to the city centre takes approximately 30 minutes.

A more expensive means of transfer to the city centre is to take a taxi. It is best to take an airport taxi rather than the regular services, as they have a cheaper flat-rate fare, rather than a surcharged meter.

In the arrivals hall at the airport there is an information office providing assistance with accommodation (Oct–May: daily 8.30am–9pm; June–Sept: daily 8.30am–11pm).

BY BOAT

It is possible to arrive in Vienna by boat along the Danube. One of the most regular operators is the Erste Donau-Dampfschiffahrts-Gesellschaft (Friedrichstrasse 7, tel: 588 800, www.ersteddsg.at). Cabins for overnight travel must be booked in advance. Bicycles can be transported with prior reservation. You can also return by the same route, or combine the trip with a rail ticket. Contact the following for other operators: Cosmos-Maritim, Kärntner Ring 15, tel: 5153 3160; G. Glaser, Handelskai 265, tel: 726 0820; Eurocycle, Schulgasse 36, tel: 4053 8730; Seereisen Center, Bayerngasse 1/23, tel: 713 0400.

BY CAR

Travelling to Austria by car from northern Europe is a long and arduous journey, best achieved by routing through Germany to take advantage of the toll-free and excellent motorway network. Beware of attempting to

> **By rail**
> There are excellent international and national rail connections with Vienna. EU train links are particularly fast. Information is available from Rail Europe, tel: 08705 848 848, www.raileurope.co.uk
>
> Arriving in Vienna from the west, you disembark at the West Bahnhof (travel office provides accommodation assistance daily 7am–10pm). From here, the No 52 and 58 trams leave for the city centre; No 18 provides a link with the South station.
>
> Austrian Railways are extremely efficient and punctual. It is possible to book tickets online which can be posted abroad (www.oebb.at).

enter the country via the less busy Alpine passes, which can be closed at night and in winter.

To reach the south or east of the city, you should leave the A1 at the Steinhäusl intersection and approach the city along the A21. (There is an information office with accommodation assistance north of the city centre exit, in Triesterstrasse.)

Apart from a valid driving licence, registration papers and a nationality sticker, you are also required to carry a first-aid kit and a warning triangle. It is also advisable to obtain international documentation from your insurance company before you set off. The wearing of seatbelts is compulsory and children under the age of 12 are not allowed in front seats.

The Austrian equivalents of the AA and RAC are the ÖAMTC and the ARBÖ. They provide a breakdown service on all motorways and main trunk roads, as well as within the city boundaries of Vienna itself. Non-members can call and pay for the service by credit card, redeemable on your insurance (ÖAMTC, tel: 120, www.oeamtc.at; ARBÖ, tel: 123, www.arboe.at).

Speed restrictions in Austria are: on motorways, 130km/h (80mph); and in built-up areas 50km/h (30mph), unless there are signs to the contrary.

Getting Around

Vienna's proverbial easy-going charm disappears when it comes to driving. Mercilessly pushing and shoving their way forwards, each driver fights their way ahead. The one-way system in the centre of the city has been specifically designed to discourage cars from entering at all. Parking spaces are rare, multi-storey garages expensive and the parking restrictions awkward.

So, don't drive in Vienna; if arriving by car, leave it on the city outskirts or at your hotel. Vienna's public transport is exemplary, comprising rail, underground, tram and bus. These have all been integrated into one system with many convenient and clearly labelled interchanges. All forms of transport arrive regularly and run late.

THE S-BAHN

From whichever direction you approach the city by S-Bahn (suburban railway), you will find interchange stations where you can transfer to the underground. Many popular destinations in the countryside surrounding Vienna can be reached conveniently by taking the S-Bahn, and then changing to the local railway system.

The Palais des Beaux Arts

THE U-BAHN

The five U-Bahn (underground railway) lines are an ideal, and easy, way of getting into and around the city centre. They are:

U1: Kagran–Stephansplatz–Karlsplatz–Reumannplatz
U2: Schottenring–Volkstheater–Karlsplatz
U3: Erdberg–Stephansplatz–Ottakring
U4: Hütteldorf–Karlsplatz–Schwedenplatz–Heiligenstadt
U5: Heiligenstadt–Westbahnhof–Meidling–Philadelphiabrücke

TRAVEL BY TRAM

Vienna's tram system is very extensive and runs to almost all areas of the city; however, the most useful lines for visitors are:

1 and 2 around the Ringstrasse
31 and 38 from Schottentor to Grinzing and Stammersdorf
52 and 58 from the West Bahnhof to the city centre

TRAVEL BY BUS

Like the trams, the bus network is very extensive. The principal lines in the city centre are:

1a: Schottentor–Stephansplatz
2a: Burgring–Graben
3a: Schottenring–Schwarzenbergplatz.

Seven days a week, there is a special night-bus service from 12.30am, when the other public transport closes down, until 4am. The buses leave Schwedenplatz along various routes marked at bus stops by a sign bearing the letter N followed by a number.

TICKETS AND PRICE REDUCTIONS

Within the central area (zone 100, or *Kernzone*) you can use a validated ticket to travel as far as you like, changing as often as necessary as long as you continue to travel in the same basic direction.

Children under the age of 6 are carried free of charge, and children under 15 pay half the adult fare. During the local school holidays (July and August) they can travel free of charge; the same rule applies to foreign children with proof of identity and age.

Tickets for individual journeys (called *Einzelfahrscheine*), and reduced tickets for children and short journeys (known as *Halbpreisfahrscheine*), can be purchased from ticket machines at U-Bahn stations, or from many Tabak stands; they must be validated immediately. Keep your ticket as inspectors do make regular checks on passengers.

A much cheaper way of getting around is to purchase a multi-journey ticket *(Streifenkarte)* for 4 or 8 journeys. This type of ticket is also more convenient if you are planning on doing a lot of travelling around the city. One strip should be validated for each separate journey. Ticket offices also sell reduced-price tickets for pensioners *(Senioren)* on the production of proof of age.

In addition, there are special season tickets at a reduced rate, which permit unlimited travel for periods of either 24 hours or 72 hours. Both tickets are valid for all forms of public transport within the central area. A Vienna Shopping ticket allows travel in zone 100 for one day from 8am to 8pm. The Vienna Card, which entitles you to reductions on admission fees to museums and galleries, is also valid for all forms of public transport for 72 hours.To purchase a season ticket for either a week or a month, you will need a passport-type photo.

Facts for the Visitor

PASSPORTS AND VISAS

European Union nationals and visitors from many other countries including the US, Canada, Australia and New Zealand do not require a visa to visit Austria. Visas are still required by nationals of some Commonwealth countries. Check before you start your holiday.

CUSTOMS

Tourists are not required to pay duty on articles brought into the country for their own personal or professional use. The following items may be imported into Austria free of customs duties: 200 cigarettes or 50 cigars or 250g

Fiacres

A fiacre (*Fiaker* in German) is a horse-drawn carriage available for hire in the city of Vienna. The name originally comes from the Rue de Saint-Fiacre in Paris, in which carriages were available for public hire for the first time in 1622. The first fiacres appeared in Vienna in 1693, when Leopold I granted the first coach hire licence. Today, there are only about 30 of them left. The drivers, who still wear traditional hats and uniforms and are known for their anecdotal and occasionally embroidered accounts of Viennese history, are amongst the most popular sights in the city. A perfectly serious suggestion made by the city administration in 1979 – that the horses should wear 'nappies' to avoid fouling the city streets – provoked a vigorous (and effective) protest by the coachmen.

Fiacres, which unfortunately come at a price, are available for hire at the Heldenplatz, in the Augustinerstrasse in front of the Albertina, and on the north side of St Stephen's Cathedral. They offer short, round trips, which last for approximately 25 minutes, or longer ones, of about 50 minutes' duration.

Bicycles
There are some 370km (230 miles) of cycle tracks within the city. ARGUS, the working party for environment-friendly urban traffic, has produced an excellent map (obtainable from bookshops) showing the cycle tracks. Good general information is contained in the brochure Discovering Vienna by Bike, which also lists cycle hire shops, and Vienna Bike, available from tourist information offices and the Vienna Tourist Board *(see below)*.

tobacco; 2 litres of alcohol (of less than 22 percent), and 1 litre of alcohol (of more than 22 percent). Citizens of EU member states are allowed to import and export much larger quantities for their own use (800 cigarettes, 90 litres of wine etc.) There are no restrictions on the import and export of local or foreign currency.

PARKING

The labyrinth of one-way streets in the city centre has been deliberately designed to deter the individual motorist. There are very few parking spaces and the rare multi-storey car parks are extremely expensive. There are also numerous parking restrictions, which are rigidly enforced. In all restricted parking areas (indicated by blue demarcations) and in all districts numbered I to IX, parking on week-days between 8am and 6pm (in some cases, as late as 8pm) is only permit-ted for a maximum of 90 minutes, and car owners are required to display a parking disc and a parking ticket – these can be obtained at public trans-port information offices, garages, tobacconists' and in some banks.

In addition, between 15 December and 30 March there is a general ban on parking between 8pm and 5am in all streets with tram lines, to facilitate snow clearance.

INFORMATION

There are a number of Tourist Infor-mation offices in the city. The two main ones are:
Information-City, Albertinaplatz/Ecke Mayseder g, 9am–7pm.
Information-South, Triestestrasse 149, Apr–Jun, Oct, 9am–7pm, Jul–Sept, 8am–10pm.

There are also information offices at main railway stations, at the airport and by the motorway exits (Auhof, Apr–Oct 8am–10pm, Nov 9am–7pm, Dec–Mar 10am–6pm). The three gov-ernment tourism websites are also use-ful: www.wien.gv.at, www.info.wien.at and www.austria-tourism.at

The Vienna Tourist Board is at Obere Augartenstrasse 40 (tel: 211 140), and there is a Stadtinformation office in the Rathaus (tel: 52550).

Transport information offices
The public transport system's infor-mation offices, which all give infor-mation on prices and provide maps, are open as follows (for all locations: tel: 790 9105):
Karlsplatz and Stephansplatz, Mon–Fri 7am–6pm, Sat–Sun and public holidays 7am–6.30pm.
Praterstern and Philadelphiabrücke, Mon–Fri 7am–6.30pm.
Volkstheater, Mon–Sat 7am–6.30pm.

SIGHTSEEING

On foot
Walks are organised through various districts of the city. There are around 25 different routes covering a variety of themes, including 'Jewish Vienna – Past and Present', 'Vienna in the Footsteps of the Third Man', 'Freud and Schoenberg in Vienna' and 'Con-temporary Architecture along the Danube'. Each tour is accompanied by a trained guide, and takes about 90 minutes to complete. Further infor-mation can be found in the pamphlet

called Vienna Walks, obtainable from the tourist information office. To book tours tel: 876 7111 or 774 8901, e-mail: office@wienguide.at Information about all the walks is available on the Wiener Spaziergänge website at www.wienguide.at

CURRENCY AND EXCHANGE

In 2002, the euro (€) became the official currency used in Austria. Notes are denominated in 5, 10, 20, 50, 100 and 500 euros; coins in 1 and 2 euros and 1, 2, 5, 10, 20 and 50 cents.

Banks are open Monday to Friday 8am–12.30pm and 1.30–3pm; Thursday until 5.30pm (main offices do not close for lunch). Foreign currency can also be exchanged at many travel agencies and on any day at the bureaux de change at the West Bahnhof (7am–10pm) and Süd Bahnhof (6.30am–10pm, November to April till 9pm only) railway stations, at the Central Post Office (Hauptpostamt), and at the Österreichisches Verkehrsbüro in Opernpassage (9am–6pm). The City Air Terminal bureaux de change is open 8am–12.30pm and 2–6.30pm, and the office at Schwechat Airport 6.30am–11pm.

By far the easiest way to get money, however, is from an ATM *(Automat)*, which are dotted across the city.

SERVICE CHARGES AND TIPS

Although service charges are often included in restaurant prices, it is customary to add about 10 percent to the total. Taxi drivers and hairdressers also expect a 10 percent tip.

MUSEUMS

Most state museums grant entry free of charge to children under 10 years of age; in municipal museums, the age limit is six years. There is a reduction for schoolchildren (with passports) and students (with international student identity cards).

For non-students, the Vienna Card (around €16) is well worth considering. This not only gives you a discount on admission fees to many of the city's museums, but also unlimited free travel by underground, bus (excluding night buses) and tram for 72 hours, and a discount on the shuttle bus from the airport to the city centre. It can be bought at your hotel, at any of the information offices, or by credit card (tel: 79844 00128).

OPENING HOURS

Usually Monday to Friday 8.30 or 9am–6pm (sometimes with a break at

Boarding the
Karlsplatz bus

lunchtime from noon until 2–3pm), Saturday 9am–noon. On Thursday some shops stay open until 8pm; on Saturday larger shops stay open until 5pm. Some major shops are permitted to remain open Monday to Saturday until 8pm (9pm in summer) and on Saturday until 6pm; those at railway stations 7am–10.30pm.

Mail

Stamps may be purchased at post offices and in tobacconists' shops. Post offices are generally open Monday to Friday 8am–noon, 2–6pm; the Main Post Office at Barbaragasse 2 and the post offices at West and Süd Bahnhof are open 24 hours.

Telephone

Telephone calls may be made from post offices and telephone kiosks. Some public telephones require the use of a telephone card, obtainable from post offices. To make an international call, dial 00 + the country code: Australia 61; France 33; Germany 49; Japan 81; Spain 34; United Kingdom 44; US and Canada 1. The code for Austria is 43 and the area code for Vienna is (0)1.

*The extremely luxurious
Hotel Bristol*

US access codes for Austria are: AT&T: 022 903 011; MCI: 0800 200 235; Sprint: 022 903014.

Important Telephone Numbers

Police: 133
Fire brigade: 122
Emergency doctor: 141
Ambulance: 144
Breakdown service: 120, 123
Chemist (out-of-hours): 1550
Emergency dental service: 512 2078
Flight information: 7007 22233
Train enquiries: 051 717
Radio taxi: 31 300, 40 100, 60 160, 81 400, 91 091
Lost property office: 313 440
Directory enquiries (local): 11811
Directory enquiries (long-distance): 11814

Diplomatic Representation

Australia: tel: 512 8580
Canada, tel: 5313 83000
Germany, tel: 711 540
Ireland: tel: 715 4246
New Zealand: tel: 318 8505
UK, tel: 7161 35151
USA, tel: 31339

Time zone

Austria is on Middle European Time, 1 hour ahead of GMT. Daylight saving applies from October to March.

ACCOMMODATION

Vienna possesses hotels in all categories. However, if you want to stay in the city centre and enjoy a reasonable degree of comfort, you will find that the prices are relatively high. Hotels are placed in three categories, for which the approximate prices in euros, per person per night in a double room, are as follows: **€€€** above €160; **€€** from €100 to €160; **€** below €100. Breakfast is usually included in the price and many hotels offer special deals for weekend breaks etc.

HOTELS

€€€

Hotel Bristol, Kärntner Ring 1, tel: 515 160, fax: 5151 6550, e-mail: hotel.bristol@luxurycollection.com Opposite the Staatsoper, the hotel's service and rooms more than match its location. Very expensive but considered one of the world's best hotels. It has a very fine restaurant.

Hotel Imperial, Kärntner Ring 16, tel: 501 100, fax: 5011 0410, e-mail: hotel.imperial@luxurycollection.com Probably Vienna's most luxurious hotel, set in a 1873 Ringstrasse palace. The rooms are opulent in the extreme and the service second to none. Like the Bristol, this is one of the world's finest hotels.

Hotel im Palais Schwarzenberg, Schwarzenbergplatz 9, tel: 798 4515, fax: 798 4714, e-mail: hotel@palais-schwarzenberg.com Built between 1697 and 1727, this Baroque palace is now an opulently luxurious hotel set in 7 hectares (18 acres) of private parkland. The rooms include a number designed by Pado Piva. There is also an excellent restaurant.

Radisson sas Palais Hotel, Parkring 16, tel: 515 170, fax: 512 2216, e-mail: sales.vienna@radissonsas.com Sensitively and cleverly converted from two 19th-century palaces into a luxury hotel, the elegant rooms have a more contemporary feel than those of the Bristol and Imperial.

Sacher, Philharmonikerstrasse 4, tel: 51456, fax: 5145 6810, e-mail: wien@sacher.com A famous luxury, city-centre hotel, home of the 'Sachertorte' *(see page 113)*. The recently renovated rooms preserve their Viennese feel, loaded with antiques and fine art works.

€€–€€€

Hilton Vienna, Am Stadtpark, tel: 717 0000, fax: 713 0691, www. hilton.com A superior member of the Hilton group, very convenient for the City Air Terminal. Geared towards conferences and business travellers.

Hotel Inter-Continental Wien, Johannesgasse 28, tel: 711 220, fax: 713 4489, e-mail: vienna@interconti.com A huge 1960s international-style luxury hotel with good service and well-maintained rooms.

Vienna Marriott Hotel, Parkring 12a, tel: 515 180, fax: 5151 86736, www. marriott.com A large glass-clad, American-style business hotel. Centrally-located on the Ringstrasse and with well-appointed modern rooms.

€€

Pension Altstadt, Kirchengasse 41, tel: 522 6666, fax: 523 4901, e-mail: hotel@altstadt.at Considerate service and imaginative, individual rooms in an elegantly and thoughtfully designed pension. Centrally located near the Volkstheater.

Hotel Astoria, Kärntnerstrasse 32–4, tel/fax: 51577, e-mail: astoria@austria-trend.at A very centrally located hotel, recently renovated with comfortable rooms and a good restaurant.

Hotel Austria, Wolfengasse 3, tel: 51523, fax: 5152 3506. Newly reconditioned rooms, some without bath that are cheaper, in an elegant, friendly and quiet hotel.

Dorint Hotel Biedermeier im Sünnhof, Landstrasser Hauptstrasse 28, tel: 716 710, fax: 7167 1503. A great little hotel overlooking a courtyard walkway lined with boutiques. As the name suggests, the decor of the spotless rooms is Biedermeier.

Hotel König von Ungarn, Schulerstrasse 10, tel: 515 840, fax: 515 848, e-mail: hotel@kvu.at A 16th-century building close to Stephansplatz containing a charming hotel established in 1815. Comfortable and traditionally decorated rooms.

Mailberger Hof, Annagasse 7, tel: 512 0641, fax: 512 0610, e-mail: reception@mailbergerhof.at Converted from a Baroque palace into a traditional, quiet hotel close to the Staatsoper.

> **👁 Youth Hostels**
> Vienna has a number of Youth Hostels, many of which are quite a way out of town (the most central is on Myrthengasse). A number are listed below; more information can be obtained from the Austrian hostelling website at www.oejhw.or.at
> **Hostel Ruthensteiner**, Robert-Hamerling-Gasse 24, tel: 893 4202, fax: 893 2796.
> **Jugendgästehaus Hütteldorf-Hacking**, Schlossberggasse 8, tel: 877 1501, fax: 8770 2632 (open all year).
> **Jugendgästehaus Vienna-Brigittenau**, Friedrich-Engels-Platz 24, tel: 3328 2940, fax: 330 8379.
> **Jugendherberge**, Myrthengasse 7, tel: 523 6316, fax: 523 5849 (open all year).
> **Schlossherberge am Wilhelminenberg**, Savoyenstrasse 2, tel: 48585 03700, fax: 48585 03702.
> **Turmherberge Don Bosco**, Lechnerstrasse 12, tel: 713 1494.

Hotel Wandl, Petersplatz 9, tel: 534 550, fax: 534 5577, e-mail: reservation@hotel-wandl.com A family-owned hotel since 1854, the Wandl is very central and has well-priced renovated rooms.

€

Hotel Kärntnerhof, Grashofgasse 4, tel: 512 1923, fax: 5132 22833, e-mail: karntnerhof@netway.at Small and friendly, this hotel has a number of loyal returning guests. Quiet but very central, the rooms are well -priced.

Hotel Kugel, Siebensterngasse 43/Neubaugasse 46, tel: 533 3355, fax: 523 1678. Excellent value, budget accommodation, convenient for transport links. The hotel has well-maintained rooms and helpful staff.

Hotel-Pension Arenberg, Stubenring 2, tel: 512 5291, fax: 513 9356, e-mail: arenberg@ping.at An excellent little hotel, right on the Ringstrasse. Comfortable rooms in an atmospheric 19th-century building. Good breakfasts and friendly helpful staff.

Pension Pertschy, Habsburgergasse 5, tel: 534 490, fax: 534 4949, e-mail: pertschy@pertschy.com A good-value and well-located pension in the Palais Cavriani. The rooms are quiet and comfortable.

Pension Wild, Langegasse 10, tel: 406 5174, fax: 402 2168, e-mail: info@pension-wild.com Great value accommodation in pleasant clean rooms. Welcomes gay and lesbian couples.

CAMPSITES

Aktiv Camping Neue Donau, Am Kleehäufel, tel: 202 4010 (mid-May–mid-Sept).

Campingplatz Schloss Laxenburg, tel: 02236 71333 (Apr–Oct).

Wien Süd, An der Au 2, tel: 888 4154 (July/Aug).

Wien West I/II, Hütteldorfstrasse 40 and 80, tel: 941 449 (15 July–15 Sept) or 942 314 (open all year).